In American History

The Battle of the Little Bighorn in American History

Nancy Warren Ferrell

E

Enslow Publishers, Inc.

44 Fadem Road
Box 699
Springfield, NJ 07081
USA

PO Box 38
Aldershot
Hants GU12 6BP
UK

To my husband, Ed Ferrell, biographer and American history buff

Library of Congress Cataloging-in-Publication Data

Ferrell, Nancy Warren.
The Battle of the Little Bighorn in American History / Nancy Ferrell.
p. cm. — (In American History)
Includes bibliographical references and index.
Summary: Describes the Battle of Little Bighorn and the events that led up to it.
ISBN 0-89490-768-9
1. Little Bighorn, Battle of the, Mont., 1876—Juvenile literature.
[1. Little Bighorn, Battle of the, Mont., 1876.] I. Title. II. Series.
E83.876.F43 1996
973.8'2—dc20 96-11592
CIP
AC

Printed in the United States of America

10 9 8 7 6 5 4 3 2

Illustration Credits: A Bailey, Dix, & Mead photo, State Historical Society of North Dakota, p. 114; © 1995 Carolyn J. Yaschur, p. 18; Colorado Historical Society, p. 35; Courtesy of Little Bighorn Battlefield National Monument, pp. 6, 11, 22, 39, 50, 67, 73, 74, 77, 81, 84, 88, 92, 94, 98, 103, 110; Courtesy of the Burton Historical Collection of the Detroit Public Library, p. 52; David F. Barry photo, State Historical Society of North Dakota, pp. 55, 64; Denver Public Library Western Collection, p. 112; Orlando Scott Goff photo, State Historical Society of North Dakota, p. 59; Reproduced from *America's Fascinating Indian Heritage* © 1978, The Reader's Digest Association, Inc. Used by permission, p. 9; © Smithsonian Institution, Washington, D.C., p. 96; State Historical Society of North Dakota, p. 106.

Cover Illustration: Courtesy of Little Bighorn Battlefield National Monument; Orlando Scott Goff photo, State Historical Society of North Dakota.

★ Contents ★

★ Acknowledgments ★

The author is especially grateful to Douglas C. McChristian, former chief historian at the Little Bighorn Battlefield National Monument in Montana, for reading the manuscript for accuracy. Also helpful was Park Ranger Kitty Deernose, who assisted with photographs.

Thanks go to the many historical societies and libraries in the United States Southwest and Northwest, particularly the Alaska State Library, the Juneau Public Library, and the University of Alaska Southeast Library in Juneau, Alaska. Plus thanks to my husband, Ed Ferrell.

Native American participation in events leading to and including the Battle of the Little Bighorn can best be remembered by words from one of their enemies.

We took away their country and their means of support, broke up their mode of living, their habits of life, introduced disease and decay among them, and it was for this and against this that they made war. Could anyone expect less?

—General Phillip Sheridan, "The Plains Indian Warrior,"
Little Bighorn Battlefield National Monument, Montana

1

A Vision of Victory

In May of 1876, a large Sioux and Cheyenne camp crowded along the Rosebud River in Montana Territory. It was a typical morning. In the distance, young boys herded horses. Nearer at hand, children darted between tepees, dogs barking at their heels. Women prepared breakfast. The savory smell of buffalo meat drifted in the air. It was a peaceful scene.

But peace was not on the mind of Sioux Chief Sitting Bull. Soon his men would fight government soldiers—the Bluecoats—who were searching for hostile warriors. Sitting Bull was preparing for war.

That morning Sitting Bull took the feather from his hair and loosed his black braids. He washed the red paint from his face. Then he picked up his long pipe and wound sprigs of sage around the stem.

When he was ready, he asked three warriors to go with him. Together they climbed a nearby hill. There Sitting Bull faced the sun, holding the pipe stem toward the sky. Then he made his prayer to the sun, asking that the Sioux nation be successful in what they were to do. Sitting Bull also promised to hold a Sun Dance, hoping a vision of the future would come to him.

Sitting Bull, a great Sioux chief, was a leader in the fight against the whites in the Battle of Little Bighorn.

In time, the Sun Dance was performed. During the ceremonies, Sitting Bull received a vision.

In this vision, the Sioux chief heard a voice from above saying, "I give you these because they have no ears." Then in his dream Sitting Bull saw soldiers dropping upside down from the sky. The Bluecoats had no ears, and their hats were falling off. The soldiers were falling into camp.

Everyone celebrated when they heard the vision, for they knew what it meant. The soldiers who would not listen to peaceful talk would come—yes. They would come, but they would be defeated! The Sioux would win a great and glorious victory.[1]

European Invasion

Early Sioux had a saying: "A people without history is like wind on the buffalo grass."[2] The heritage of Sitting Bull and of all Native Americans goes back thousands of years.

When Europeans stepped upon the North American continent in the late 1400s, they found people already there and named them Indians. (The European explorers thought the ships had sailed to the country of India.) These Native Americans lived different lifestyles and spoke different languages, often communicating through sign language. No one knows for sure, but around the year A.D. 1500 close to 5 million Native Americans lived in what is now the United States.[3]

2

RIDERS OF THE PLAINS

Before the white adventurers arrived on the North American continent, very few Native Americans lived on the Great Plains between the Mississippi River and the Rocky Mountains. Before the explorers, "the Indians had lived as farmers and small-time hunters on the fringes of the plains, doing their work and traveling afoot."[1] Native Americans' only pack animal, the dog, could neither go very far nor carry heavy loads. Because of this, few tribes lived on the Plains.

Early European Influences

The arriving Europeans who brought horses and guns in the late 1400s changed much of the Plains lifestyle. In the decades after, through trading and stealing, tribes obtained horses. By the 1800s, Plains hunters like the Sioux, Cheyenne, Crow, Blackfeet, Comanche, and Kiowa tamed wild horses and rode them expertly.

What a difference the horse made, especially on the Great Plains of America. It actually created a new life-style for Native Americans—as wanderers. Whereas a tribal camp might move six miles a day using dogs to

Indian: Rub left hand, back and forth, twice

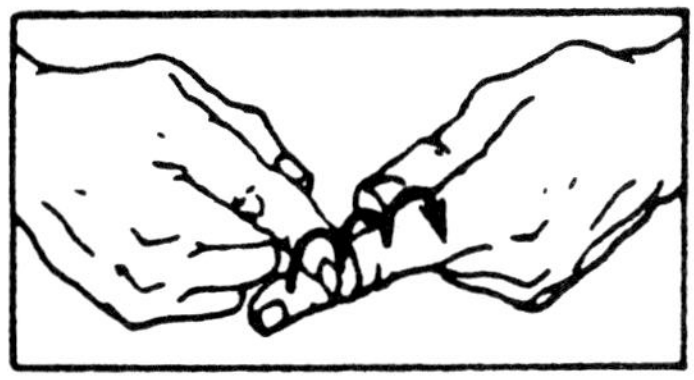

Cheyenne: Chop at left index finger

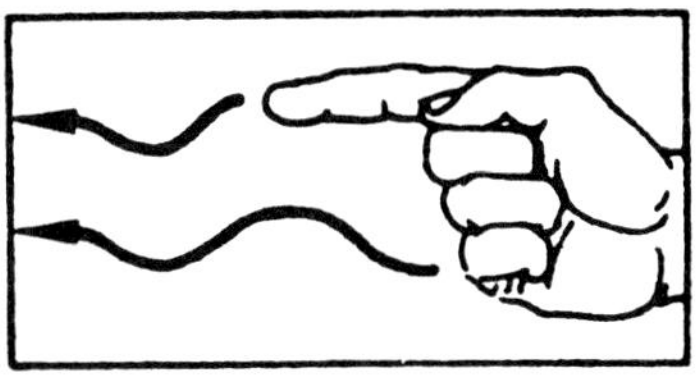

Comanche: Imitate motion of a snake

Crow: Hold the fist on forehead, palm out

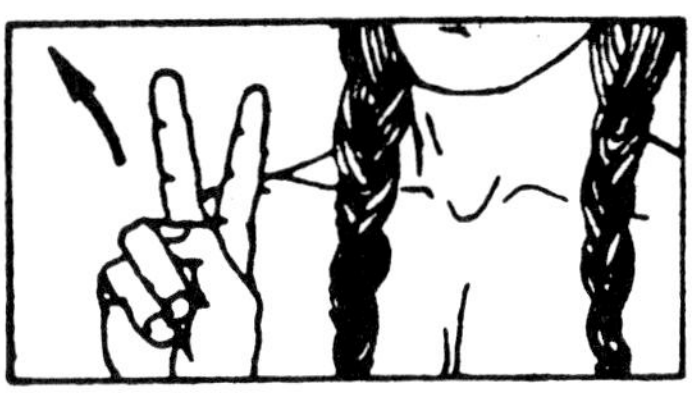

Pawnee: Make V-sign and extend hand

Nez Perce: Move index finger under nose

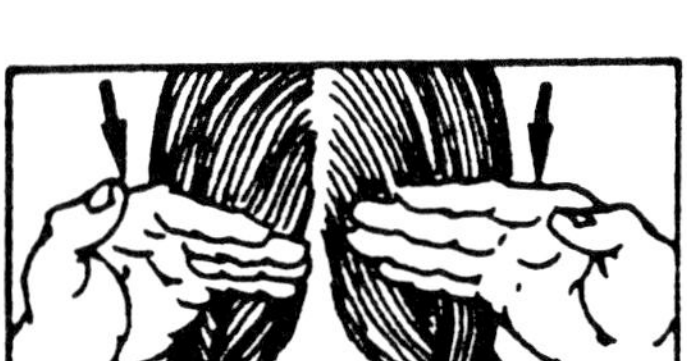

Osage: Move hands down along back of head

Sioux: Hand across neck in cutting motion

Even though many tribes did not speak the same language, they often communicated in sign language. Here are signs for particular tribes. Oddly, the sign for "Indian" was always used first, before identification.

pull loads, a camp with horses could travel thirty miles in an emergency.[2]

Warring and raiding against other tribes proved a basic part of Native American life. The reasons for raiding might be for revenge, for horses, for plunder, or in defense of tribal territory. It was not a game, but serious business.

A major change brought by the horse dealt with a primary food of the wandering tribal bands—the buffalo. These huge animals supplied just about everything for the Plains family.

Before the horse, warriors stalked buffalo on foot. Hunters tried to hide from the animal and kill it by surprise. Or they stampeded the animals over a cliff, then killed them as they lay injured below. The horse enabled riders to travel farther from camp in search of buffalo. Because of the enormous number of buffalo herds ranging the Plains, people were able to put a supply of food away for leaner times.

The Plains tribes became dependent on the buffalo. A large buffalo supplied enough meat to feed a hundred people.[3] What was not eaten was used for something else—clothing, moccasins, tepees, bed covers, game equipment, riding and transportation gear, weapons, tools, and utensils. Its blood was used for paint, its hooves for glue, and its hair for pillows.[4] Even the dried droppings of the beast—buffalo chips—fueled fires when wood was not available. Because of these many gifts, tribes held religious ceremonies to honor the animal. Buffalo proved the

Because of the introduction of the horse, Native Americans began to hunt buffalo more efficiently. This drawing of a buffalo chase is by George Catlin.

one source from which stemmed the people's very existence.

Along with the horse, Europeans also introduced guns to America. On average, a warrior could shoot twenty arrows in the time it took to load and fire a musket gun once. Yet they saw the advantage of the noise, smoke, surprise, and effectiveness of the weapon. Tribes were quick to adopt them. The combination of horse and gun made the Plains rider an impressive fighter.

The horse and the buffalo provided these people with an independent, roving Plains life. Other than enemy tribal territories, there were no boundaries on land. It was a mobile, free existence.

But as the explorers, mountain men, miners, adventurers, soldiers, and white settlers moved ever westward across the country during the mid-1800s, the buffalo began to disappear. The buffalo roamed in herds ranging from five to fifty, and sometimes hundreds of thousands of animals covered the hills.[5] The buffalo supported the economy and influenced the warfare, religion, and society of the Native Americans. This animal, the very essence of Plains life, was fast disappearing.

SIOUX FAMILY GROUPS

The Sioux were made up of closely related tribes:

Lakota, Teton, or Western Sioux:

- Oglala
- Brulé
- Hunkpapa
- Sihasapa
- Miniconjou
- Oohenonpa
- Itazipco

Nakota or Middle Sioux:

- Yankton
- Yankonai
- Hunkpatina
- Assiniboine

Santee, Dakota, or Eastern Sioux:

- Mdewakanton Tribe
- Wahpeton Tribe
- Wahpekute Tribe
- Sisseton Tribe

The Sioux language family consisted of different groups with various histories and lifestyles.[6]

Cheyenne and Sioux were only two of many tribes that hunted on the Great Plains of America. The Cheyenne were divided into northern and southern groups while the Sioux were divided into several groups.

The life of these Plains people was different from that of the invading white society. The reasons for war were also different.

For the tribal individual, the primary goal of warfare was to show bravery.[7] To touch an enemy—called a *coup*—was an honor credited to the warrior. The touch was made at close range either with the hand, a stick, or by a weapon such as a knife, club, or spear. Hitting an enemy with an arrow was a coup, as was touching a dead enemy. However, it was braver to touch or kill at close range, where the combat was riskier. Counting as many coups as possible gained status for a warrior. The warring of white soldiers did not have that focus on individual achievement.

These kinds of individual combat—for personal glory and for the group—made the fighting unpredictable. Companions never knew exactly what one another would do. And certainly the enemy did not. It was difficult, if not impossible, for an enemy to plan an attack against that kind of guerrilla, or individual, warfare. Such unpredictability worked well against the United States Army in the battles that came later.

Actual warfare methods were different between Native Americans and Europeans, too. Generally, Plains riders fought in loosely organized groups under an informal leadership. Warriors—mostly men, but on rare occasions women—were not required to follow a leader. A warrior looked to the most experienced leader to follow as long as the leader was successful. Or a warrior rode out on his own, looking for chances for personal bravery. An individual was not bound to orders or by strict discipline within the tribe.

Warfare by whites was different. The soldier normally fought not for personal glory, but for pay and for the honor of his uniform. In a general sense, military armies planned ahead and fought in groups, depending on firepower and superior numbers.[8] Soldiers followed strict orders and a line of command according to rank. The army "persisted in using tactics and organization adapted from European textbooks that contained no useful hint on how to employ troops against Indians."[9]

Another difference between Native American and European cultures dealt with land ownership. Europeans believed a person could buy property, build a fence around it, farm it, sell it, and leave it to relatives.

Native Americans could not understand that thinking. To them, land was community property, used by everyone. It was to be used and cherished; land was often referred to as the Earth Mother. Older people even believed that by sitting on the earth or by walking barefoot on the soil, one could absorb the earth's strength or its healing powers.[10] Most of the tribes agreed, "One could no more own the earth and its bounties than hold a monopoly on sunshine and rain."[11]

As more Europeans arrived on eastern shores, differing images grew in both cultures. Natives were not civilized, some whites said. They needed the Christian way of life. They needed education. Hunting was "wild," and the natives needed to be tamed, and trained in the farming lifestyle. Native Americans were often called "noble red men" or "blood thirsty savages."[12] Still other whites did not care about Native Americans at all. The whites needed the land, and the natives were in the way.

On the other hand, the Native Americans resisted that philosophy. They had been living on the continent for thousands of years. After all, *they* were the hosts, and the Europeans were simply invaders, greedy land-grabbers. Whites were liars, some said. They broke promises and were not to be trusted. The Native Americans wanted to keep their religions, their languages, their lands, and their lifestyles.

Until the mid-1800s, the cultures clashed as settlers and adventurers moved ever westward. Eventually, battles erupted on the southern, central, and northern Plains of America. Native Americans from each of these areas would be among the warriors participating in the battle along the Little Bighorn River on the grassy hills of Montana.

3

Treaty Talk and Broken Promises

Before the 1800s, most white people living east of the Mississippi River thought the land west of it was a desert. What good is that wasteland, they asked. Nothing was there but buffalo and sagebrush.

But as wagon trains broke trails to Santa Fe and immigrants crossed the wasteland on their way to Oregon, eastern people began to change their minds. They found fertile valleys beyond the Mississippi, and animals of many kinds. And when gold was found in California in 1848, the immigrants flooded west. In 1850 alone, fifty thousand gold seekers traveled past Fort Laramie, Wyoming, on the way to mines in California and Oregon. They left behind "dying grass, thousands of dead buffalo, deaths among Indians and white alike from hunger and from the cholera that the wagon trains brought with them."[1]

By 1850, Native Americans on the central Plains knew the buffalo were disappearing: The animals were harder to find. As a result, some tribes—especially the Cheyenne who lived more directly in the path of the immigrants—slowly starved.

The tribes fought back against this invasion, attacking travelers and wagon trains crossing their hunting grounds. By mid-century, the government in Washington could no longer sit back and ignore the problems between white travelers and the Native Americans. Since the government could not control the roving tribes, they would instead try to bargain for a peaceful settlement.

Treaty of 1851

One of the people trying to deal with problems on the plains was Thomas Fitzpatrick. Fitzpatrick, a former mountain man, was an agent for the United States government. He was stationed at Fort Laramie in Wyoming Territory, along the Oregon Trail. The Native Americans called him "Broken Hand," because he was missing three fingers due to a rifle explosion.[2]

Fitzpatrick took his job as an agent seriously, trying to protect the tribes from whiskey peddlers and dishonest travelers. But as time went on and waves of white traffic crossed the Plains, he could envision more problems. He saw the buffalo disappearing and pictured more troubles. Trying to prevent bloodshed, the government asked Fitzpatrick to call a meeting of the Plains tribes to see if everyone could come to an agreement.

With professed good intentions,[3] United States officials proposed drawing up a treaty. Treaties are agreements between nations where each side gives something and receives something in return. In the

The Native Americans of the Plains depended heavily on the buffalo to support their lifestyle. Unfortunately for those tribes, the buffalo were quickly disappearing by the middle of the nineteenth century.

Treaty of 1851, Native Americans were asked to agree to certain conditions in exchange for money, food, and other supplies they could not otherwise obtain.

Fitzpatrick then sent runners up the Platte and Missouri rivers, along the Yellowstone River, and over the Bighorn Mountains in Wyoming. These runners invited chiefs of many tribes to Fort Laramie to talk over the problems. The government promised blankets, guns, and food if the bands came.

In September 1851, ten thousand Native Americans camped in a grassy valley close to Tom Fitzpatrick's agency near Fort Laramie. Among the bands were Sioux, Crow, Cheyenne, and Shoshones. More tribes crowded near the fort than had ever assembled in a single spot before.[4]

The groups arrived with caution since their enemies were arriving too, and all were mistrustful of the council. Some bands, such as the Kiowa and Comanche, did not come at all because they were afraid their horses would be stolen. Soldiers stationed at the agency helped keep peace: One wrong incident could mean disaster for the entire conference.

In the end, Sioux, Cheyenne, Arapaho, Crows, Assiniboine, Gros-Ventre, Mandan, and Arikara signed the Treaty of 1851. These tribes agreed to allow whites to build roads and forts across their lands; they agreed to accept boundaries in which to live; and they agreed to no longer fight among themselves. The areas within the assigned boundaries were called territories in this treaty. In other treaties they had already been called reservations—land reserved for the tribes.[5] Eventually, the term changed from territory to reservation. The government not only intended to clear the natives away from white travel routes, but also to assign them to specific areas. An area within these boundaries—one per tribe—guaranteed a tribe's hunting ground and homeland. Whites and other tribes were not to enter these areas.

Tribes still kept their right to pass over, hunt, and fish in lands outside their reservation area.[6] Indeed, hunters often had to leave their reservation in pursuit of buffalo and other game. Tribes could live on land outside reservations, but they had to avoid white travel routes.

In turn, the government would supply the natives with protection, money, and thousands of dollars worth of trade goods, domestic animals, and agricultural tools. The tribes would receive annuities, or payments, of fifty thousand dollars a year in goods (blankets, beef, flour, etc.) for fifty years.

The whites who signed the 1851 agreement intended to clear natives from white travel routes and off white settlements. They also expected to contain them within a certain area. The treaty, then, meant that a Sioux could not raid an enemy Crow camp—the Sioux was not even permitted to step on Crow land. The Cheyenne could not race over the grassland in search of buffalo, for they had to respect treaty boundaries. By outlawing raiding, horse thieving, and warring, the treaty did away with some of the activities at the core of tribal life. It did away with activities that brought honor and authority to both an individual and a group.[7]

Another important effect of the treaty dealt with dependence. By furnishing bands with hunting ammunition, food, and items they could not get elsewhere, the government set itself up as a provider. The goods included items individuals enjoyed—like sugar and coffee—and for which they had developed a taste. In order for people to obtain such items, they had to go to the agencies, or frontier trading stores, run by government men.

The Native American signers of this document could hardly have understood it fully. First, no one member, according to tribal organization, had the authority to speak for all the people.[8] A chief might sign the treaty, but he could not force his will upon other band members. His written mark on a treaty, or his pledge, did not bind others to his thinking. Second, cultural and language differences affected the interpretation of the document.

However, Oglala Sioux Chief Black Hawk had a good idea of what the treaty meant. He knew the relationship between Native Americans and whites when he said, "You have split my land and I don't like it. These lands once belonged to the Kiowa and the Crow, but we whipped these nations out of them, and in this we did what the white men do when they want the lands of the Indians."[9]

When the signed treaty and the council report were returned to the government in Washington, D.C., the Senate reduced the length of the annuity to ten years. Officials did not consult the tribes. And when the native leaders returned to their homeland after the council, they threw away the agricultural tools they received at Laramie. So the Treaty of 1851 failed even before it became law: One side changed the terms of the treaty; the other side ignored them.

Although they did not want them, Native Americans saw the necessity of trading posts. This trader's store was in Fort Yates, Dakota Territory.

Result of the Treaty of 1851

In due time, the Treaty of 1851 went into effect. Forts went up along travel routes. The government built agencies where the people picked up their annual money and government supplies. Such agencies were usually built near the forts, but not always.

The U.S. Indian Bureau employed government agents like Tom Fitzpatrick to make sure supplies were distributed properly. An agent set the tone. A good one—and they were rare—was respected, and the government plan operated fairly. A bad one could cause frustration and resentment among the tribes. At one post, for example, a new agent arrived only to find that the man he was replacing had not been seen at the agency for a month. There was no money there, only unpaid bills. And the nearby tribes had not received annuities for four years![10]

Furthermore, the government supplies sent west for the Native Americans were often of poor quality, or they were not the type of food or supplies families were used to. Typically, the promised supplies never even arrived; they were either stolen by dishonest agents or sent to the wrong post. When this happened, people often starved.

By the early 1850s, tribesmen had grown dependent on hunting with ammunition and firearms supplied by white traders. These dealers set up shop in or near the forts or along the rivers. Natives looked with mixed feelings on such traders. They were necessary and unwanted at the same time. Although many Plains people wanted white supplies, they did not want the traders crossing their land, steaming down the rivers, cutting trees for fuel, or allowing their stock to eat prairie grass. More crippling were the diseases traders brought and the whiskey they supplied. The natives had no immunity against either.

The next few years after the Treaty of 1851 proved difficult for the Plains people. This was true particularly for the Cheyenne, who lived more directly along the white transportation routes. As Tom Fitzpatrick wrote in a report, they were in "want of food half the year, and their reliance for that scanty supply, in the rapid decrease of the buffalo [was] fast disappearing."[11]

Still, a steady flow of white immigrants continued traveling through Plains country. In various incidents, whites and Native Americans confronted each other. The situation on the Plains grew worse.

Then an incident occurred in the summer of 1854. Actions of an arrogant army officer, Lieutenant John L. Grattan, fueled hateful emotions on the Plains.

Near a trading post east of Fort Laramie in Wyoming, a Sioux warrior named High Forehead killed an ox led by a Mormon settler. When the story came out, Sioux Chief Brave Bear offered to pay for the dead animal. The offer was refused.

What happened next is not clear. Apparently, Grattan, the new lieutenant from West Point stationed at Fort Laramie, was bored and ached for action. He decided to arrest High Forehead. The 1851 Laramie treaty stated that Native Americans and whites should punish their own for crimes against one another. A soldier trying to settle the score acted against the law. However, Grattan convinced his commanding officer to let him have thirty men to march to the Sioux camp and arrest High Forehead.[12] Along with this troop Grattan hauled two short cannon.[13]

When Grattan and his troops reached the Sioux camp where High Forehead hid, there was more talk. Again, Brave Bear went back and forth between the camp and the troopers, trying to keep peace. The

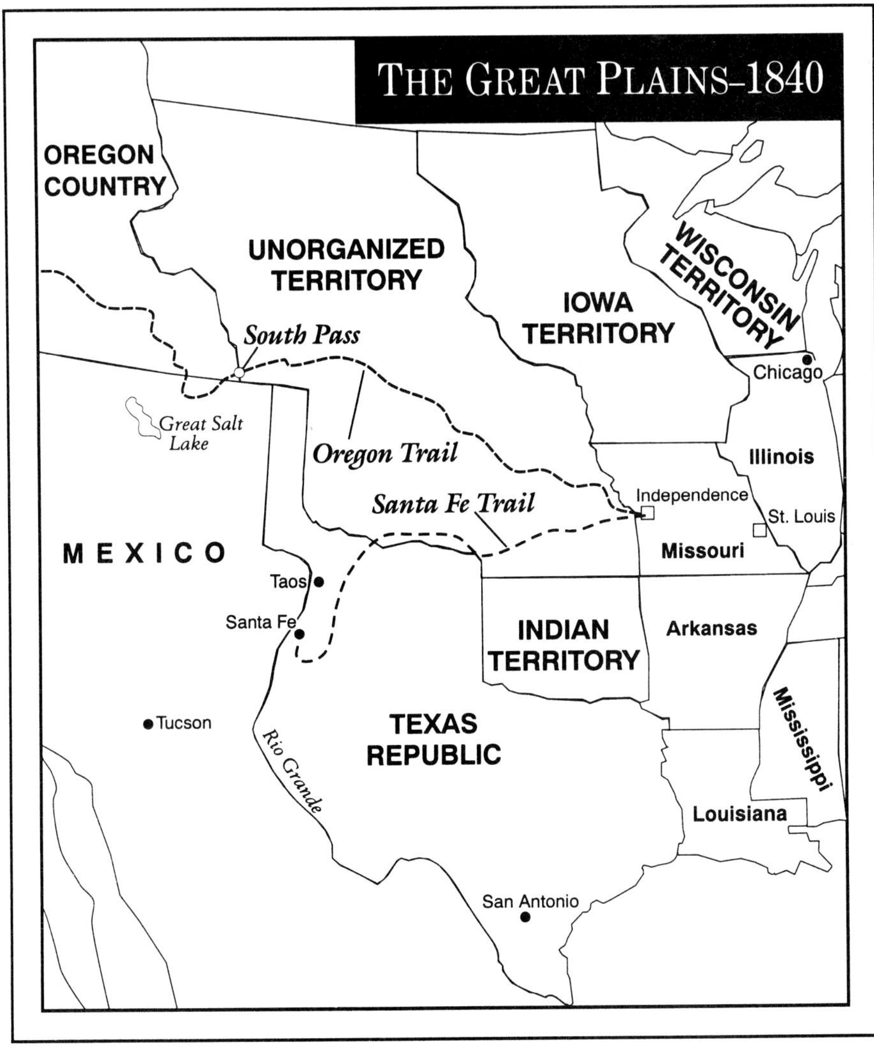

This map shows the Great Plains in the 1840s. Today, this area covers the states of Texas, Oklahoma, and New Mexico.

Sioux would not give up High Forehead, and the troopers refused payment for the ox.

No one is sure what happened next. Bullets flew through the air. Grattan's men fired their heavy artillery. Shots tore through the tepees, and Brave Bear died in the crossfire. Sioux warriors swarmed forward and killed all but one of the soldiers. The conflict was over in minutes. For the first time, blood of American soldiers was shed upon the Plains.[14]

The lone survivor, Private John Cuddy, either escaped and hid or was helped by the Sioux. He made it back to the post and later to Fort Laramie, where he died.

There was further retaliation from the soldiers after that. In fact, this crisis sparked revenge and counter-revenge. Series of clashes continued between whites and Native Americans for nearly thirty more years.

The Treaty of 1851 said that whites would not be allowed on tribal land, but that promise was broken. During the summer of 1856, the government sent an engineering expedition onto Native American land near the Black Hills. At that time the area was called Dakota Territory. Later it would be divided into North and South Dakota. The hills rose in the western section of what is now South Dakota. A Sioux chief stumbled upon the whites and warned them to leave.

First Grand Council

Alert to white expansion, the northern Teton Sioux (also called Lakota) called a grand council of their own during the summer of 1857. An estimated seventy-five hundred Lakota gathered at the northeast section of the Black Hills.[15] Among the numbers were the outstanding warriors who would later fight for the Sioux homeland.

The Hunkpapa Sioux named Sitting Bull (1831–1890) was there. He was about twenty-six years old at the time. Sitting Bull had been born near Grand River in what is now South Dakota. He had grown to be a well-respected warrior, singer, and healer. Later, in 1867, Sitting Bull would become the only man ever to be honored as principal chief of the entire Sioux nation.[16]

Also attending the council was a nineteen-year-old Oglala Sioux warrior, Crazy Horse (1838–1877). Born along the banks of Rapid Creek near the Black Hills, Crazy Horse was a loner and a fierce warrior. The focus of his life was to protect the Lakota and their lifestyle and to keep the Black Hills for his people.[17]

Already a skilled warrior and leader in his thirties, Oglala Sioux Red Cloud (1822–1909) attended the meeting. Red Cloud had been born along the Platte River in Nebraska Territory. As he grew older, he developed skills of political and military leadership. His unyielding attitude toward the whites at that time mirrored the feelings of his fellow Lakota.[18]

At this council, the Lakota bands pledged their unity and promised to keep white people from their lands.

Gold in Colorado

While the Sioux tribes survived in the north, ever more Europeans flowed across the central Plains. Prospectors in Colorado discovered gold in 1859, and miners built their camps on Cheyenne land. Between 1858 and 1862, eighty thousand immigrants moved onto tribal land in the mountain region.[19] They were not just moving across land designated for the Plains people, they were settling on it. The city of Denver began growing, becoming a center for the Rocky Mountains.

While a network of thirty thousand miles of railroad track patterned the East,[20] a debate raged for years about whether a railroad could cross to the Pacific Ocean. Several routes were explored, the most logical running through Salt Lake City, Utah, and on to Sacramento, California. On July 1, 1862, Abraham Lincoln signed the Pacific Railroad bill into law. This bill gave permission to build one railroad going east from California and another one going west from mid-continent. The tracks would eventually meet, connecting the United States from east to west—the first transcontinental train system. Completion would bring still more people to the Plains country.

Several other events in the early 1860s encouraged whites to travel west. The transcontinental telegraph, completed in 1861, linked messages from Washington, D.C., to San Francisco in seconds. Then in 1862, Abraham Lincoln signed the Homestead Act, which offered citizens and those who intended to become citizens public land on which to settle.

With so many people coming to and passing through the Plains, many Native Americans reacted. They fought.

The United States government, though busy with the Civil War in the East, tried to keep peace with the Native Americans. Officials bought sections of the prairie from the various tribes, shrinking their land piece by piece. That, along with the disappearing buffalo and the increased railroad travel, only added to growing tribal frustration.

Among those resisting the white invasion were the Cheyenne. Some of them would fight later at Sand Creek. Still others would join Sitting Bull for the ultimate fight at Little Bighorn. But while the Cheyenne skirmished on the central Plains, a conflict in Minnesota between whites and Santee Sioux attracted public attention there.

4

PRESSURES EXPLODE

If tribal bands on the Plains felt the pressure of whites crossing their hunting areas, Sioux cousins farther east were even more pressed. The Dakota (Santee Sioux) tribe of Minnesota had already experienced a generation of white families settling in their area, taking land. There the two cultures had been surviving with an uneasy peace.[1]

However, one year the promised food and supplies from the government did not arrive. After a winter of near starvation, an isolated incident set off an explosion of killing.

Minnesota Massacre

In August 1862, a few resentful Santee braves killed five settlers. To support the braves and vent years of frustration, Dakota war parties struck. They raided and massacred almost every white person in sight. Those whites who had been particularly abusive to the Dakota received special treatment. One target was storekeeper Andrew Myrick. When the Dakota's credit at the store had run out earlier that summer, Myrick had refused to give food to the hungry people.

He had said, "If they are hungry, let them eat grass."[2] When the storekeeper's body was found after the killings, Myrick's mouth was stuffed with grass.

More than four hundred settlers died before the killings stopped.[3] In the end, the Dakota were subdued. However, many of them fled west into Montana's Powder River country.

Some of the Dakota who fled joined Sitting Bull's people. The Lakota had been camping along the Little Missouri River in western North Dakota. The Dakota reported soldiers were coming up the Missouri by the thousands.

Until then, the Lakota, of which Sitting Bull was a member, had not worried too much about white travelers going through their country. There had not been many up to that time. However, with the discovery of gold closer to home in Montana in 1861, the few white travelers became many. Miners soon trailed through in droves, both by land and by the Missouri River. A mere two years after the discovery, Virginia City, Montana, sprang up. Stampeders rushed there to dig silver and gold from the area. Resentment for these intrusions was building.

The Bozeman Trail

In 1862, a trailblazer named John Bozeman broke a route through the northern Plains into the goldfields of Montana. This route branched off from the Oregon Trail, then followed through northern Wyoming, and into southwestern Montana. From there it crossed several major rivers—the Powder, the Tongue, the Bighorn, and the Yellowstone. Eventually, it led to Virginia City, Montana. The route was called the Bozeman Trail. It passed through prime buffalo country, west of the Black Hills.

The story of the Bozeman Trail is an example of similar events experienced by settlers and natives on other westward trails. The northern Plains, including the Black Hills, was one of the last outposts of the Sioux. Through the years that followed, raids on white travelers became routine.

The Black Hills country was not only beautiful to the tribes—it was also sacred. Native Americans believed it to be a home for religious spirits. For the Lakota and Sitting Bull, the Black Hills were also a food source, a kind of storage of small animals: When the Lakota needed food, they could always go there and hunt.[4] By the terms of the Treaty of 1851 signed at Fort Laramie, the Black Hills were saved for the natives' hunting grounds. While the agreement insured tribal rights in the area, the United States government also said it could build roads and military posts in these territories. However, the Native Americans thought the treaty said that white people would stay out of the area. There was no real problem until gold was found in 1861.

Clashes between Sioux and whites occurred when miners and traders began flowing over the Powder River–Bozeman Trail into gold country. Red Cloud's warriors, the Oglala Sioux, harassed travelers constantly. Red Cloud was ambitious, haughty, and a skilled warrior. He was determined to protect his people and to hold on to his warrior ways.[5]

While conflicts continued on the Bozeman Trail, attention soon focused on the central Plains and the southern Cheyenne. Some of these tribesmen would eventually join in the Little Bighorn fight years later.

Slaughter at Sand Creek

During the later years of the Civil War, in 1864, the situation grew worse on the Plains. In an effort for natives to save their land and for whites to use and obtain the same land, each side fought the other. Although treaties had been signed, many of their provisions were not honored. Settlers in growing numbers continued to travel over and settle on reserved land.

There were attempts at peace. Cheyenne Chief Black Kettle (1803–1868), in particular, tried to live according to the soldiers' instructions. Black Kettle's tribe believed that they remained under the protection of the United States government. The chief persuaded his people to live in peace.

Not all tribes, however, took that view. The warring faction of the Cheyenne held no mercy for the ever-increasing flow of white travelers. Warriors attacked supply trains, wagon trains, and white settlements. Once they isolated Denver, Colorado, to the point where no mail arrived for a week. People of Denver gasped at the stories of atrocities other white people told. For instance, in June 1864, only thirty miles from the city, two white settlers and their two children were scalped and cut up. Their remains were brought into Denver.[6]

The governor of Colorado, John Evans, finally declared war on the hostiles. He authorized the territorial military commander, Colonel John Chivington, to win that war. Chivington, a former Methodist minister and now fired with political ambition and racial hatred, was called the Fighting Parson.[7] He had no sympathy for the natives. Chivington organized a short-term volunteer army, with men enlisting for a hundred days. It was formally the Third Colorado Cavalry but nicknamed the Hundred Dazers.[8] The regiment was formed mostly with rowdies from the mining camps and from the streets of Denver.

Cheyenne Chief Black Kettle still looked for peace in spite of the unrest around him. On September 28, 1864, he and other Cheyenne and Arapaho leaders met near Denver with Evans and Chivington. They were assured of peace if they moved close to one of the nearby forts. In November, Black Kettle and six hundred followers did just that: They made camp at Sand Creek along the Arkansas River. The village stood about forty miles from Fort Lyon in southeastern Colorado. Other peace-minded bands joined Black Kettle there.

To Chivington, the months following the meeting proved too peaceful. The hundred-day enlistment for

SOURCE DOCUMENT

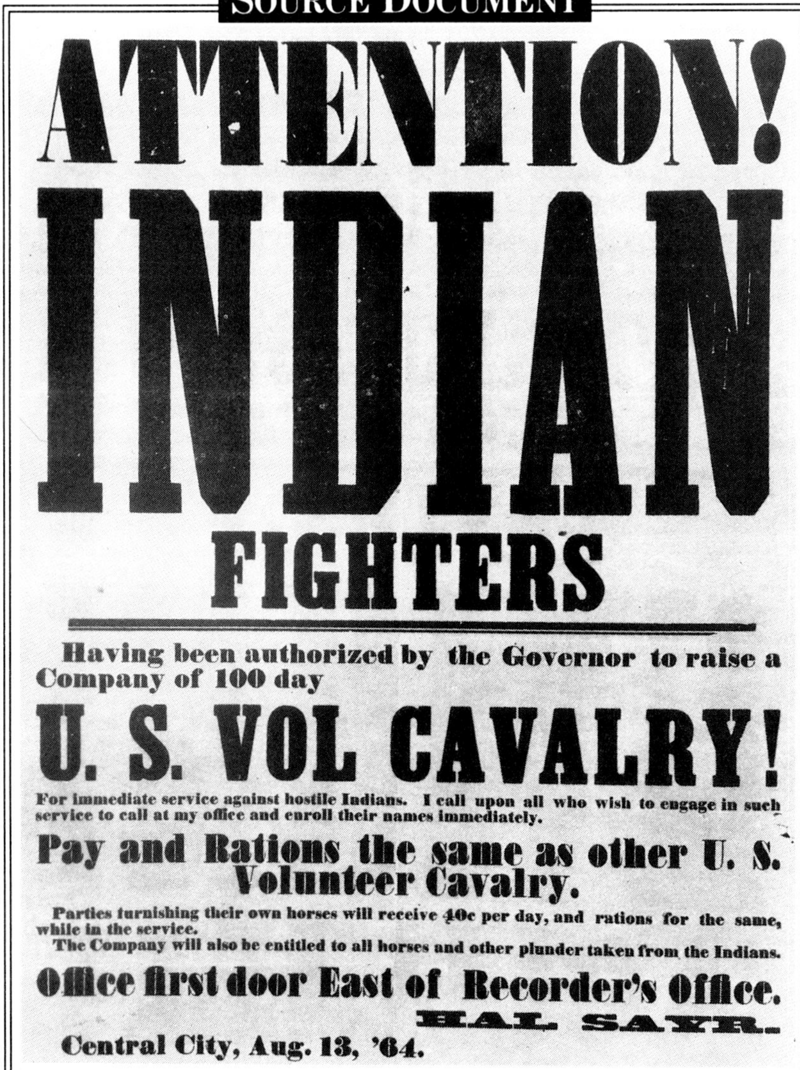
ATTENTION!

INDIAN

FIGHTERS

Having been authorized by the Governor to raise a Company of 100 day

U. S. VOL CAVALRY!

For immediate service against hostile Indians. I call upon all who wish to engage in such service to call at my office and enroll their names immediately.

Pay and Rations the same as other U. S. Volunteer Cavalry.

Parties furnishing their own horses will receive 40c per day, and rations for the same, while in the service.

The Company will also be entitled to all horses and other plunder taken from the Indians.

Office first door East of Recorder's Office.

HAL SAYR.

Central City, Aug. 13, '64.

This poster recruited volunteers to fight the Native Americans in Colorado. These volunteers were nicknamed the Hundred Dazers because of their hundred day term of enlistment.

his cavalry was almost up, and there had been no fighting. Either the Third Colorado Cavalry had not encountered the enemy, or they could not find them. A few people in Denver began making fun of the Hundred Dazers, and Chivington knew his political support was falling. He decided to do something about it. The colonel knew where one large Cheyenne camp stood—peaceful or not. Chivington vowed to kill natives, one way or another. Sand Creek was his target.

Chivington and his troops rode through deep snow and arrived at Fort Lyon on November 28. There the colonel discussed his intention of attacking the peaceful Cheyenne camp. The plan shocked the soldiers. Chivington posted a guard to be sure no one left the fort to warn the enemy.[9]

That night, Chivington's volunteer troops, about seven hundred strong, marched from Fort Lyon. With them they trailed four small cannon.

By dawn, they were in sight of Black Kettle's camp at Sand Creek. Before the attack, Chivington told his men: "Kill and scalp all, big and little; nits make lice."[10]

Since they were in a peace camp, the Cheyenne posted no guards. The camp was composed of about five hundred people, most of them women and children. The men were in hunting camps about fifty miles away.

Chivington surrounded the camp without calling an alarm. The Cheyenne were soon aroused, however.

Black Kettle quickly raised an American flag on a lodgepole and immediately followed it with a white flag of surrender. People crowded under the flags. Black Kettle assured them they were under the protection of the United States government. When shooting started, the people fled.

The soldiers fired pistols, rifles, and cannon. They rode through camp, killing anyone alive. They scalped and mutilated men, women, and children, showing no mercy. People hid any place they could. Black Kettle and his wife escaped. She was shot nine times but survived.[11]

Two hundred Cheyenne, most of them women and children, died during the massacre.[12] By nightfall, the troops had withdrawn, leaving hidden remnants of Cheyenne. Together, in zero-degree weather, the survivors made their way on foot toward the hunting camps in the north.

Meanwhile, Chivington and his troops paraded in triumph through the streets of Denver. They displayed over one hundred scalps to a theater crowd. For a while the men were heros—until the truth surfaced. Then the massacre and its participants were looked upon with disgrace. Even the army's judge advocate general called the Sand Creek massacre a "cowardly and cold-blooded slaughter."[13]

The public and the press in the East found the massacre at Sand Creek sickening. Congress set up three different investigations and worked to revise a new policy toward the Native Americans.

Out West, if there had been trouble with the

Plains tribes before, now there was rage like no other. Sioux and Arapaho joined the Cheyenne in a great council and smoked the war pipe. One member said, "We have now raised the battle-axe until death."[14]

During the next several months, the Cheyenne sought revenge. They killed scores of settlers and hunters, burned stagecoach stations, and destroyed telegraph lines. The situation grew so inflamed that eight thousand troops were pulled from the Civil War and sent west to keep order.[15] The incident at Sand Creek more than ever convinced the Native Americans that white men, or certainly most of them, could not be trusted.

Black Kettle and eighty families, still hoping for peace, retreated south of the Arkansas River to a small camp. The warring tribes knew the army would send troops against them. They decided to leave the area and join their northern Sioux and Cheyenne friends in Powder River country.[16]

Sioux chiefs, among them Sitting Bull and Red Cloud, heard the news of Sand Creek, which flashed from tribe to tribe. The massacre only added to the growing war sentiments. The Sioux of Powder River welcomed their allies.

Warrior numbers on the northern Plains were growing.

The Laramie Council of 1866

In the North, raids against white travelers along the Bozeman Trail in Powder River country became

Red Cloud played an important role in leading his people in a war against the United States government.

everyday happenings. The government finally decided there had to be some agreement for use of the trail. United States Commissioner E. B. Taylor, the government's negotiator, called for a council at Fort Laramie to try for a peace policy. Possibly because of the growing poverty of his people, Red Cloud decided to attend and see if they could come to an agreement.

The council consisted of Red Cloud, other chiefs, and government commissioners. They met in early June 1866 at Fort Laramie, Wyoming. After some bargaining, it seemed that peaceful use of the trail might be negotiated if game in the area were not disturbed. Taylor said nothing about the forts to be built along the Bozeman Trail. Instead, he focused on the money, goods, and guns the tribes would receive for hunting, and on leaving them alone to their hunting grounds.

As the peace council talked, an infantry column headed by Colonel Henry B. Carrington marched into Fort Laramie. The colonel announced to the group that he was on his way into Powder River country to build forts on the Bozeman Trail to protect travelers.

When Red Cloud heard that, he exploded. "The Great Father sends us presents and wants us to sell him the road," he stormed, "but White Chief goes with soldiers to steal the road before the Indians say Yes or No."[17] Red Cloud rode off and half the chiefs went with him. As a warning, the departing Sioux jammed a pole into the trail and tied a piece of red cloth and a lock of hair to it. In Plains terms, that meant "Turn back or die!"[18]

Spotted Tail, a Brulé Sioux and uncle to Crazy Horse, still had hopes for peace. He stayed and signed the treaty with several lesser chiefs.

The Bozeman Trail Turns Bloody

The Laramie Council of 1866 settled matters for some of the peaceful tribes, but Red Cloud and his followers saw it as a betrayal. After the meeting, Red Cloud's warriors swooped down on white travelers with even more vengeance. The trail became known as the Bloody Bozeman.

In the end, Colonel Henry Carrington built the three forts on the Bozeman Trail: Fort Phil Kearny, Fort C. F. Smith, and Fort Reno. When they were completed, the real Sioux harassment began. Warriors, particularly under Red Cloud, cut off the mail routes, attacked wagon trains, and set upon soldiers sent out from the forts to gather wood. There were other trouble spots, too.

Forts afforded some protection, but at times it was necessary to leave their protective walls. Those venturing out were open to attacks by Sioux and Cheyenne, often headed by Chief Red Cloud.

Colonel Carrington erected Fort Phil Kearny on a key position of the Bozeman Trail. It was a large post, near a source of water, overlooking a long portion of the trail. The only problem was that the fort was several miles from timber, which the soldiers needed for construction and fuel. Therefore, a small troop had to take a wood wagon train out and back every day. Each day Red Cloud's warriors attacked. Only a relief detachment from the fort chased them away.

In November 1866, Captain William Fetterman rode into this situation to join the regiment. He was a born fighting man who looked with contempt upon Native Americans. He believed they could not stand up to a trained military soldier. Fetterman boasted that, with eighty men, he could cut through the entire

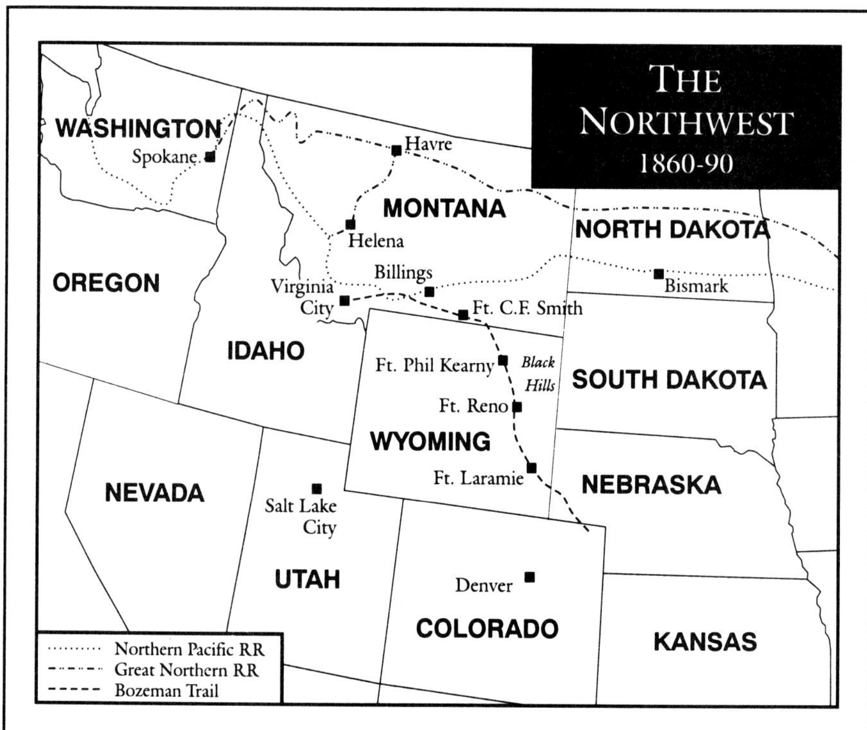

After Fort Philip Kearny, Fort C.F. Smith, and Fort Reno were built, the Sioux increased their harassment of travelers on the Bozeman Trail.

Sioux Nation.[19] He gained a chance to prove it at the end of the year.

The Fetterman Fight

December 21, 1866, was a cold, clear day. As usual, the wagon train left the fort in the morning. At 11:00 A.M. it was charged by the Sioux, led by Chief Crazy Horse. Inside the fort, Carrington ordered a relief to the rescue. This time Fetterman insisted on going out. He rounded up equal numbers of infantry and cavalry. Several civilians begged to mount up and go along, making the total about eighty men. By coincidence this was the same number Fetterman had boasted he needed to crush the Sioux Nation.

As the rescue detachment rode out of the fort, Carrington issued orders to Fetterman. The captain was to relieve the train but not to chase the enemy. "Under no circumstances," Carrington repeated, "[shall you] pursue the enemy beyond Lodge Trail Ridge!"[20]

As Fetterman and his troop neared the train, the Sioux broke off their attack. Crazy Horse moved off a short distance and boldly dismounted. Casually he checked a hoof on his horse. All this time a few other warriors rode back and forth, taunting and teasing the soldiers. It must have enraged Fetterman, for he kept his infantry in pursuit. Finally the cavalry caught up, sweeping past the infantry and over Lodge Trail Ridge. The soldiers hurried down the hill onto the Bozeman Trail and the flats of a creek.

On the other side of the ridge, hidden in gullies, were hundreds of Red Cloud's men. Not a sound did they make. They even held the nostrils of their ponies to keep them from whinnying at the sight of the army horses. After a long wait, the Sioux heard a shot—the signal that soldiers were coming. When the soldiers flowed over the ridge and into the trap, hails of arrows met them. So many arrows, an Oglala Sioux said later, that they looked like grasshoppers falling on the soldiers.[21]

Fetterman's worst nightmare rose from the grass: two thousand Sioux, cries screaming from their throats, arrows streaming from their bows. All was confusion. Some soldiers ran out of ammunition, and the warriors overran them. Others fled for cover, but they did not hold out long. Sioux numbers along with their guerrilla combat soon won the day. The entire battle was over in forty minutes.[22] It was "the worst defeat yet suffered by the U.S. Army [by] western tribes."[23]

In the fort, Carrington heard the first shots and knew something was wrong, but no one could see the battle. The colonel sent a detachment out to investigate, warning them to skirt the battle itself. The detachment finally found a viewpoint and watched from three miles away. Only when Red Cloud's men disappeared did the soldiers go down to collect the dead.

Near panic ruled inside the fort. With the Fetterman troop gone and the second relief force still out, the fort was practically defenseless. Carrington prepared for the worst should the warriors attack the fort.

That night Carrington sent for reinforcements from Omaha, Nebraska. An army scout called "Portuguese" Phillips rode all night through a blizzard to take Carrington's dispatch down the Bozeman to headquarters at Laramie. When he received the news, General William Sherman, a top army commander, responded with rage. "We must act with vindictive earnestness against the Sioux even to their extermination, men, women and children," he said.[24]

The soldiers called the fight the Fetterman Massacre. The Sioux, however, called it the Hundred-Soldiers-Killed Fight,[25] and they rejoiced in their victory.

The Sioux continued with further raids along the trail. One intense battle occurred in August 1867, at Fort Phil Kearny. In this fight, the weapons made a big difference.

The Wagon Box Fight

On August 2, 1867, civilian workers rode about six miles away from the fort to gather wood. A detachment of twenty-seven soldiers accompanied them. At the camp, as a precaution, soldiers placed fourteen large, heavy wooden wagon boxes end-to-end on the ground. This formed a type of circling corral.

When Red Cloud's warriors were spotted at about 7:00 A.M., the encamped soldiers and workers crawled into the wagon boxes. There were thirty-two men in all. Besides revolvers, all had rifles of some kind. But breech-loading Springfield rifles, which were fast and could fire long distances, had replaced the old muzzle-loaders. This change of weapons made a big difference.

During about five hours of fighting, six different waves of attack pounded toward the corral. The Sioux and Cheyenne—mostly on horseback—charged in close and then swerved away. Reports said that Red Cloud's men fought with bows and arrows and a mixture of firearms. Guns fired continually. A civilian who experienced the fight said he had a full canteen of water when the fight began, and he used most of it to cool his guns.[26] After about five hours, relief arrived—soldiers and a cannon from Fort Phil Kearny.

The number of attacking tribesmen has been estimated to be between four hundred and three thousand.[27] Three whites died, and an estimated four hundred warriors were killed or wounded.[28] This time the victory went to the soldiers.

There were so many problems along the Bozeman Trail that Congress tried again to clear the travel routes and send tribes to reservations. On July 20, 1867, the government established a peace commission. The commission met in September at North Platte, Nebraska. This location was about three hundred fifty miles southeast of the Powder River country of Montana. Several Sioux tribes attended—but few from the Power River. Spotted Tail was there, and he told the reason for all the attacks. "We object to the

Powder River road. The country which we live in is cut up by the white men, who drive away all the game."[29] The message was clear. Leave us alone.

After the commission withdrew, General Sherman responded. "The railroads are coming," he said, "and you cannot stop [them] any more than you can stop the sun or the moon. You must decide; you must submit. This is not a peace commission only; it is also a war commission."[30]

However, battles on the Bozeman Trail did not stop. Constant harassment by warriors on the trail continued. These disturbances, plus the fact that there was a railroad being built farther south, finally convinced the government to leave Fort Phil Kearny. On July 31, 1868, the Bozeman Trail was abandoned, along with the fort.[31] Red Cloud's warriors rode in victory through the empty fort and burned it to the ground. Red Cloud was the first Native American leader in the West to win a war against the United States—and he was also the last.[32] The northern Powder River region was once more tribal land—at least for the time being.

5

Setting the Scene

All was fairly quiet on the central Plains until the summer of 1867.

In command of the Plains division of the United States Army was the Civil War hero William Sherman (1820–1891). Sherman commanded the army from 1869 until 1884.

Sherman's chief lieutenant in the West was also a Civil War hero, Philip Henry Sheridan (1831–1888). Sheridan later succeeded Sherman in the Plains command. Both leaders believed in total war against any enemy they fought—and in this case, it meant the Plains tribes.

A military expedition rode to the central Plains to make a show of power and to clear the area of warring enemies. Those natives who bothered white travelers and settlers had to be dealt with.

Commanding the troops was Major General Winfield Scott Hancock, a Civil War officer. Under his command was another Civil War veteran, George Custer, who was twenty-seven years old.

George Armstrong Custer (1839–1876) grew up in Ohio and attended the United States Military Academy at West Point, where he graduated last in his class. However, during the Civil War, Custer rose so quickly in the ranks that he was dubbed the Boy General. He charged into battle both fearlessly and recklessly. He won so many victories during the Civil War that he grew very confident, thinking himself indestructible—"Custer's Luck," people called it. He demanded discipline from his men, but he was not always disciplined himself. Acquaintances said ambition drove him, and he gloried in the light of newspaper headlines.

Admiring Custer from closer at hand was his devoted wife, Elizabeth (Libbie) Bacon Custer (1843–1933). The two were married in February of 1864. Libbie accompanied her husband from post to post out West, making comfortable homes for him. When he was away, she wrote long letters to her dear "Autie," as she called him. They had no children.

On the central Plains during that summer of 1867, United States army troops did not make a good showing. The Sioux and Cheyenne rode fearlessly across Kansas, evading the soldiers. Custer pursued, but he never really caught them. It was an aimless search. Finally the campaign ended, the troops exhausted.

Since the various tribes were not brought to bay, the government in Washington, D.C., decided another peace movement was in order. The government would, it hoped, negotiate to move these tribes to reservations north of Nebraska and south of Kansas, leaving the transcontinental travel routes clear for the railroad.

More Treaties

Through the 1860s, it was clear that the earlier treaties were not working: Whites invaded tribal land; Plains warriors fought back with raids against stagecoaches and settlements; soldiers retaliated.

Tribes on the Plains noticed that the buffalo were disappearing. Wholesale slaughter of the animals began in the 1860s with the building of the railroads. The first railroad to cross the continent was linked at Promontory, Utah, on May 10, 1869. Upon the completion of the railroad, and into the 1870s, special trains were reserved for the sport of killing buffalos. Armed with guns and repeating rifles, sportsmen shot at buffalo herds from train windows, leaving wounded

George, Elizabeth, and Tom Custer spend time on their tent porch at Fort Hays, Kansas, 1868.

and dead animals along the way. Between sportsmen and buffalo hunters, the Plains were often littered with rotting carcasses and bleaching buffalo bones. The railroads, in turn, made money hauling tons of these skeletons back East, where they were processed into fertilizer and carbon.

It is difficult to grasp how fast the buffalo disappeared. In 1800, there were an estimated 60 million buffalo out West. By 1870, that number had been reduced to 13 million. And by 1900, the turn of that one century, there were fewer than one thousand buffalo left in all of the West![1]

What this did to the Native Americans, especially the Sioux and Cheyenne who depended on the buffalo for life, was predictable. With no food or other items from the buffalo, tribal families were reduced to severe poverty. Because of this, bands had to rely on the food and supplies provided by the United States government. To receive those, the people had to stay on reservations and live by government rule. It was that or starve. As General Phil Sheridan said of the buffalo hunters, "They have done more in . . . two years . . . to settle the vexed Indian question, than the entire regular army . . . in the last thirty years."[2]

With sources of food drying up, tribes went to agencies for promised supplies. But there was often not enough for everyone, or they were of poor quality. Treaty promises on both sides were ignored.

Because of these conflicts, the government urged a new round of treaties. The government aimed at

This mountain of buffalo skulls will be ground into fertilizer.

"redressing the grievances of the plains tribes and persuading them to accept reservations north of Nebraska and south of Kansas, thus abandoning altogether the corridor containing the principal transcontinental travel routes."[3]

Two treaties were negotiated and signed—one at Medicine Lodge Creek, Kansas, in 1867, and one at Fort Laramie in the spring of 1868. In the Laramie Treaty of 1868, Powder River country would be "unceded Indian territory" where no white man could set foot without Sioux consent.[4] All South Dakota as we know it today west of the Missouri River, including the Black Hills, would be designated the Great Sioux Reservation.[5] The tribes were to stay on the reservation and consider it their home; they could leave only to hunt. They were not to obstruct railroad construction or bother military posts.

In return, the government would establish an agency to supply reservations with clothing and rations for thirty years. The government would further provide schools, blacksmiths, teachers, and physicians. In turn, the Native Americans were required to make a living through farming. The government expected to help with food while families changed from wanderers to farmers.

The tribes "did not understand very clearly what they had signed."[6] By signing, they had surrendered the way of life they had followed for centuries. In addition, many tribes considered farming—the planting and gathering—as women's work. They also realized later that when they had "touched pen," or signed the treaty, they had given up the Platte River homeland country. They now had to move closer to the Missouri, a place outside their traditional hunting range. When Red Cloud, for one, found this out, he was furious.

Red Cloud was not present when the treaty was signed originally, but he did travel to Fort Laramie in November of 1868. He stated that his reasons for coming were to trade and gain weapons to fight the Crow. He said he enjoyed hunting and did not see the necessity of giving it up to farm. Only when the officer in charge told him he would receive no ammunition did Red Cloud sign the treaty. After that, he made a long speech saying that the Sioux had no intention of giving up their way of life.

The Laramie Treaty of 1868 was taken north to Powder River country and Fort Rice. A missionary was entrusted with the document and sent to Sitting Bull's camp. Sitting Bull stated his side—whites should leave Sioux land—and the missionary tried to talk the Sioux into signing the treaty.

Living in the same camp was war chief Gall (1840—1894), a Hunkpapa Sioux who was twenty-eight years old. Sitting Bull sent Gall to Fort Rice with these instructions: "You go down there and see what they have to say. Take no presents . . . Tell them to move the soldiers out and stop the steamboats; then we can have peace."[7] Sitting Bull would not budge an inch, and neither would many other leaders.

General William Sherman knew talking would not bring the Sioux to reservation life or to the reservation. "To labor with their own hands or even to remain in one place militates with all the hereditary pride of the Indian," he observed, "and *force* must be used to accomplish this result."[8]

If force was to be used, George Custer was ready to use it. He was eager to recapture the glory he had experienced in Civil War battles. Custer had his chance in 1868, farther south on the Plains, among the Cheyenne.

Hunkpapa Sioux leader Gall later played an important role in the Battle of Little Bighorn.

Southern Cheyenne, both the peaceful and the warlike tribes in the Kansas area, had been promised guns and ammunition for hunting by the United States peace commissioners. Black Kettle, the peaceful chief, believed white forces would eventually win in the West. He was ready to take his people to live on the reservation. On the other hand, warring Cheyenne Chief Tall Bull raided and harassed white settlements during the year. Because of these raids, General Philip Sheridan decided that something had to be done against the Cheyenne.

At the best of times, as Custer had discovered, it was difficult locating Cheyenne camps during most of the year. The area they roamed was large, and the soldier force looking for them was small. Tribes were usually on the move, and they knew the land well.

General Sheridan found the winter a beneficial time to attack. Native Americans rarely fought then because it was difficult for horseback riders to move on the frigid, flat, exposed prairie. In addition, their horses found little food for grazing during the cold months. Winter, for them, was just not conducive to fighting. Normally they located a concealed, protected hollow along a river and congregated there for long periods during the cold months.

Battle of the Washita

Right before Thanksgiving in 1868, Sheridan set his deadly winter campaign into action. One column of the campaign was in the command of George

Armstrong Custer. The troops were to find and destroy the Cheyenne camp that had survived Sand Creek four years before.

On a bitterly cold day, the Seventh Cavalry started, with Custer's hunting dogs in the lead. The troops were searching far south in what is now western Oklahoma.[9]

A few days into the trek, scouts located a fresh trail and brought the news back to Custer. The soldiers made a Thanksgiving meal of hardtack (a hard, flat biscuit) and coffee, then cautiously moved out. To make faster progress, the supply train was left behind. By 9:00 P.M., Custer was gazing over a hill, looking down on a herd of ponies, a half-mile away. Scattered below, among the bare cottonwood trees along the Washita River, was the Cheyenne village.

Custer divided the command into four squadrons. They were to make their silent way to positions surrounding the village. The attack would come at Custer's bugle signal, right before dawn.

There was no talking among Custer's squadron that night on the ridge. No stamping feet, no thumping chests to keep out the cold. Everything was breathlessly quiet.

The troopers might have been discovered that night if the Cheyenne guard, Double Wolf, had been awake. But the night was cold; the soldier army was far away, Double Wolf thought; and his lodge was warm. Instead of sentry duty, he fell asleep.[10]

Before dawn, Custer and his squadron mounted

their horses. Custer did not send out scouts to see the size of the camp or to estimate the number of enemies. Instead, the troops readied revolvers and repeating rifles.

Just as the men were ready for the bugle call, a rifle shot rang from the village. The bugler signaled, and the band struck up Custer's favorite march, the Irish song "Garry Owen." The musical instruments froze at once, but no matter.[11] The attack had begun. Soldiers swooped down on the quiet village.

The fighting lasted one hour. By then the Cheyenne had scattered or died. Chief Black Kettle and his wife were among the dead. The startled Cheyenne who fled had regrouped; they were joined by Cheyenne and Arapaho bands from other camps in the Washita valley. The soldiers soon found themselves facing a counterattack that was growing in size.

Custer dismounted his men, forming a half circle around the camp, and fired until ammunition nearly ran out. At that moment a four-mule wagon driven by Major James Bell and loaded with ammunition dashed through the line. With these fresh supplies, the soldiers charged and drove off the Cheyenne. From then the village was theirs.[12]

While Custer held his position throughout the day, his men torched the camp, burning tepees and their contents. Other soldiers killed the horses so their enemies could not use them again. Nine hundred ponies were shot over a period of an hour and a half.[13]

At the end of the day, Custer and his men boldly

Elizabeth Custer is standing next to Indian scout "Goose" in back row. George Custer is sitting on the bottom row center. The scene is outside Custer's quarters at Fort Abraham Lincoln.

marched toward the other camps down river. The banners flew, the band played. Then, under cover of night, the troops slipped from the valley and back to Camp Supply.

Custer had ridden from the field without searching for a small detachment of missing soldiers. The missing men had ridden from view, and the main body did not know what had happened to them. Later, they were found dead by a returning troop.

One hundred and three Native Americans and twenty-one United States soldiers (including the missing detachment) died. Custer's favorite stag hound, Blucher, was also killed. The Battle of the Washita was the first successful United States military campaign against the Plains tribes. However, it was only the first battle for Custer, who would later move north, among the Sioux.

Further Events on the Plains

About the same time as the Washita battle, a peace commission met in Chicago. At the meeting, General Sherman and his supporters decided to stop dealing with the Native Americans as independent nations. That way, the tribes could be treated as wards of the United States government. Further, the commission decided to overturn the treaty provision that allowed Sioux to hunt in "unceded Indian Territory." Instead, they were to be moved to a permanent reservation, where they would have to stay.

On the Plains, the winter of 1868–1869 was a hard one. Game was scarce, and Red Cloud's people half starved. The chief tried to obtain trading privileges with Fort Laramie, but the officers there refused, hoping to force Red Cloud onto the reservation. By spring, Red Cloud had to beg the Laramie commander for food for his people.

The end of the 1860s passed with both sides holding firm. By October 1869, almost half of the Sioux tribes (about ten thousand people) had complied with the Laramie Treaty of 1868. They were living on the reservation around the Missouri River forts and agencies at Grand River. Red Cloud lived outside the reservation, and Fort Laramie was closed to him.

Red Cloud Travels East

Finally, in April 1870, the head of the United States Indian Bureau, Commissioner Ely Parker, invited Red Cloud and Spotted Tail to visit the United States capital city of Washington, D.C. The commissioner hoped to arrive at some peaceful settlement with the leaders. Both chiefs accepted.

Who knows what went through the chiefs' minds as they rode what they called the iron horse (the train) through Omaha and Chicago, as they saw the farms and cities of America. Perhaps that was the government's purpose: to overwhelm the Sioux chiefs. Officials wanted to impress the chiefs with the size and power of the United States.[14]

Once in Washington, D.C., the chiefs were taken on a tour. In the National Armory, they saw more guns in one building then they had ever seen before. The navy paraded for them. They witnessed a display of artillery and cannon firepower set up for the visitors.

After a week, the chiefs were invited to a White House reception, where they met President Ulysses Grant. Spotted Tail kept his sense of humor through the evening. While munching on ice cream and strawberries, he mentioned to his friends that the whites ate much better food than they sent out to the Sioux.[15]

Even in Washington, D.C., the two sides could not come to an agreement.

Although Red Cloud talked with passion, he was impressed with the cities of the East. He grew discouraged. In speaking with the secretary of the Interior he said, "Our nation is melting away like the snow on the sides of the hills where the sun is warm, while your people are like the blades of grass in the spring when the summer is coming."[16]

Finally government officials compromised and said the Sioux would not have to move to Missouri. They could instead "receive their goods in the western part of the reservation at new agencies whose precise location would be selected later."[17] Red Cloud had won an important point for his people.

When Red Cloud arrived home in Sioux country, he received a mixed welcome. Some of the young warriors deserted him, believing the white people of the East had put bad medicine on him. Red Cloud, however, defended himself and his followers. Although he and Spotted Tail had made more compromises, they had not given everything away.

Some of the families eventually did try farming, but with little success. The peaceful tribes received limited supplies, but other provisions of the treaty did not appear.

Sitting Bull watched all this from a distance. As the greatest warrior of the Sioux bands, he had been elected as war chief, leader of the entire Sioux nation.

Red Cloud tried to persuade Sitting Bull to leave the warpath.

Sitting Bull would have nothing to do with compromise or reservation living, and he looked with disdain on those who did. "Look at me," he said, "and see if I am poor, or my people either. . . . You are fools to make yourselves slaves to a piece of fat bacon, some hardtack, and a little sugar and coffee."[18] Thus, renegades followed him and fought against the white invasion.

But some families did not have any choice. By this time—the early 1870s—as many as one million buffalo were being killed each year. Without government rations, the Sioux would starve. The government agency was becoming a permanent part of Sioux life. There was also pressure from the East to open reserved land to settlement or mining.

For all the importance of the Laramie Treaty of 1868, white people paid little attention to it. The Northern Pacific Railroad pushed westward through the country in 1870, and a road to Bismarck was opened in 1873. These constructions clearly violated the Laramie Treaty.[19] Several new forts were also constructed. Warriors made hit-and-run attacks on these invaders, but the government provided military escorts to protect the forts.

More Forts and Soldiers

In the spring of 1873, civilian engineers traveled to Yellowstone River country in northern Dakota

Territory to plan a route for the Northern Pacific Railroad. Since there were hostiles in the area, the Seventh Cavalry under George Armstrong Custer and several companies of infantry accompanied them for protection. Custer established Fort Abraham Lincoln as his major post in the area.

By that time, there were hundreds of forts in the West. The accommodations varied from poor to lavish. Fort Abraham Lincoln was one of the better ones.

Forts were constructed on level areas where there was a water supply, plenty of grass for the livestock and horses, and timber nearby for fuel and building. Because forts afforded protection of transportation routes through enemy country, they were isolated and far from civilization. Tribes seldom attacked a fort directly, but they raided cattle and horses grazing nearby, in spite of guards.

Enlisted men usually lived in crowded,

A winter shot of Fort Abraham Lincoln, near the banks of the Missouri River.

uncomfortable barracks, while officers fared better, many living in houses. When possible, officers' wives, like Libbie Custer, came along and made life more pleasant for their husbands.

What were those soldiers like, those men who would soon see battle? Custer had always enjoyed a reputation as a fierce fighter, but were his men of the same mold?

The cavalry troopers and infantry soldiers in the West were a different breed from those before and after. Many men were former soldiers who had served in the Civil War. Others joined the military simply to stay clothed and fed. Many joined for safe passage to the frontier out West—and its gold and excitement. Still others were criminals who found the army a good place to hide. There were the faithful and honest, too. The men were of various nationalities, almost half of the enlistees in the army being born in foreign countries such as Ireland and Germany.[20]

A great number of those troopers were new recruits. In fact, about one third of the Seventh Cavalry then were raw recruits. Many had little if any training, and some had no training at all. Others, even in the cavalry, had never before been on a horse! Fully half the officers had never, ever, fought Native Americans in which there was real resistance.[21]

The troopers certainly could not know what they were facing. Not only were the Native Americans excellent horsemen from childhood, but they were raised to be warriors. They would be impressive foes whatever their numbers or lack of weapons.

Besides regular army soldiers, regiments were usually guided by friendly Native American scouts. These guides knew the land, knew their enemies, and were skillful trackers. The Crow and Sioux, for instance, were enemies who fought over hunting grounds along the Powder River. Crow scouts, like other scouts, joined troopers either for pay or for revenge against their tribal enemies. Sometimes, for whatever personal reasons, a scout (a Sioux, for example) might join the Bluecoats and work against a fellow Sioux.

Black Hills Expedition

In the summer of 1874, Custer and his soldiers were ordered to conduct an expedition into the Black Hills. The men were to look over the land. They were to suggest where a proposed fort might be constructed, and where a military road might be built from Fort Abraham Lincoln to Fort Laramie. That would mean a route into the heart of the Sioux Reservation.

Although this invasion was against the law, United States General Alfred Terry was in favor of it. Terry, who headed the army's Dakota District, said the government had been sending military exploring companies into unceded territory for a long time, and that was all this expedition was.[22] Of course the Black Hills were not unceded territory, as Terry said, but untouchable Sioux reserve. Expedition plans went ahead anyway.

Custer suspected the government wanted him to find signs of gold. If gold were found, stampeders would come and overrun the land in spite of the Native Americans. Therefore, Custer asked to take a geologist along. The government agreed.

With a flourish, on July 1, 1874, the expedition started. Custer's bay horse pranced from the fort, Custer

Custer led the 1874 Black Hills Expedition in search of gold. This wagon train is passing through Castle Creek Valley.

in the saddle, banners flying, forty hounds yipping on the ground. Behind him were one thousand men, one hundred ten wagons, three rapid-fire Gatling guns, a sixteen-piece band, one hundred Arikara scouts, a pack of reporters, and a professional photographer. In the group was Custer's brother Tom, President Grant's son, and the grandson of the telegraph inventor Samuel Morse.

The expedition did find gold in the Black Hills. Not much, but enough. Custer summoned his favorite white scout, "Lonesome" Charley Reynolds,[23] to take the news through dangerous country to Fort Laramie.

Reynolds quickly prepared. He cleaned his rifle. Out of leather and sponge he made footgear that would not make a sound or leave a trail. Then he stuffed food in a pack, strapped a blanket to the saddle, and took off with the dispatch.[24] Reynolds raced through dangerous Sioux country, traveling at night and hiding during day. He made it to Laramie with the news to be telegraphed to the world.

Meanwhile, Custer returned to Fort Lincoln on August 30.

The mere hint of gold sent fortune-hunters stampeding to the Black Hills, unmindful of anything else.

The Sioux, especially those connected with the agency, complained about the invasion of "Long Hair" Custer and his soldiers into their territory. The Black Hills were sacred and tribes resented the invasion of their land. The intrusion only added to the growing anger against the whites.

Anyone familiar with the Treaty of 1868 knew the provisions. The military was to protect the tribes and prosecute any violator who wronged them. And "no white person or persons shall be allowed to settle upon or occupy any portion of the same; or without the consent of the Indians . . . to pass through the same."[25] Yet here were stampeders crossing reserved land in total disregard of the treaty. General George Crook and his troops tried to keep the prospectors out, but the miners were too many and the soldiers too few.

Because of this invasion, there was some fighting, with the promise of much more to come. In the end, Washington, D.C., officials ordered the tribes living in gold regions to transfer to other lands. This ruling was in direct opposition to the treaty. By so ordering, the purpose of the military in the area changed from protecting the Native Americans' land as originally authorized to protecting the white gold stampeders. The tribes were commanded to obey the order.

Over the next year and a half, more white adventurers arrived. By the fall of 1875, an estimated eleven thousand miners packed into the Black Hills.[26]

6

Crook's Arm of the Little Bighorn Campaign

In 1876, the United States celebrated its 100th birthday of the creation and the signing of the Declaration of Independence. In that period of one hundred years, the population in the United States had grown from 3 million[1] to approximately 44 million people.[2] The population of Native Americans during the same period dropped from about one million to an estimated three hundred thousand.[3] Disease and warfare proved the major causes. The northern Plains was like an island surrounded by a sea of people. It seemed to be the only place in America left almost unoccupied by white people. The interests of both the Sioux and the government focused on the Black Hills.

The federal government wanted to buy the Black Hills, but the Native Americans refused to sell. Red Cloud, who had seen the strength of the white man, was open to negotiation. Other leaders, including Gall, Sitting Bull, and Crazy Horse, would not consider a compromise. When officials in Washington, D.C., found that the natives would not give in, they issued a command: All tribes of Dakota and in the Wyoming Territory were to return to their agencies by the end of January 1876, or they would be considered "hostile." The army then would drive them back. Government officials thought the threat would frighten the roving bands.

Over the next months, the tribes learned of this order. They had not been planning wholesale war, and they did not know what to make of the command. Time itself—like the calendar date of January 31, 1876—had little meaning for them.[4] After all, they were an independent people, hunting freely as they had for generations. Besides, that winter was an especially cruel one. Time was not spent on traveling, but in surviving the zero degree temperatures and blowing winds.

Sitting Bull knew peace would not last. In March, he was reported saying he would fight the whites to keep his free life.

Lieutenant General Philip Sheridan was in command of the army on the north and south Plains. It was Sheridan's responsibility to force the Native Americans back onto the reservations. He devised a three-prong plan to accomplish that aim.

General Sheridan's plan was simple. Three columns would converge from three directions on an area thought to be occupied by hostile tribes.[5] General George Crook (1829–1890), with more than one thousand men, was to go north from Wyoming country toward Montana. General Alfred Terry (1827–1890) commanded two columns: the Dakota, which he headed; and the Montana Column, headed by Colonel John Gibbon. Terry, with Custer and 925 soldiers, was to march west from Fort Abraham Lincoln in Dakota Territory toward the Yellowstone River in Montana. Colonel John Gibbon (1847–1896), with 450 infantry and cavalry troops, was to advance east from western Montana Territory toward the Yellowstone River. The idea was to put the rebels in a vice between these forces and defeat them.

From the South with General Crook

General George Crook, who headed the southern arm of the campaign, had been an officer in the Civil War. Later he commanded troops fighting tribes out West. According to William T. Sherman, commander of the Missouri Division of the army, Crook was "the greatest Indian fighter and manager the United States ever had."[6] He was considered most effective fighting the hostile Apaches in Arizona.

Crook was effective but eccentric, riding to war on a mule and wearing unusual clothing. Warriors called him Three Stars, perhaps because they observed a star on his hat and one on each shoulder.[7] As a person, Crook was considered decent and compassionate. He saw his native enemies as humans rather than as savages

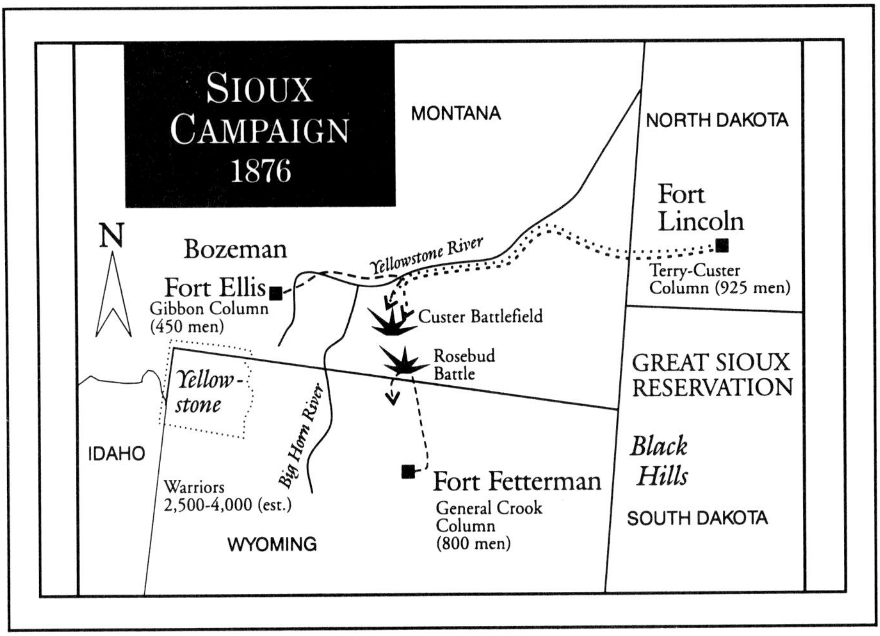

This map illustrates General Sheridan's plan. General Crook's troops moved north, while General Gibbon led his men east then south, and Custer's troops headed west then south.

to be destroyed. His soldiers enjoyed serving under him, and they thought of him affectionately.

Although Sheridan wanted a winter campaign, only one of his striking columns managed to gear up and assemble before the winter was over. In March 1876, General Crook prepared to move his troops into the Dakota country. There he would search for hostiles not living on the reservation. Weather on the Plains was cold and harsh. Crook soon understood why the tribes "had been so reluctant to leave their winter camps."[8]

The troops set off in bitter cold. On March 16, a

General George Crook was considered an eccentric but caring and fair commander.

scout reported locating a small Cheyenne and Sioux village on the Powder River. That night Crook sent Colonel Joseph Reynolds with three battalions to attack the camp at dawn. Crook and his soldiers would meet them later, after their victory at the Powder River.

Reynolds' calvary attacked the village the next day. At the charge, the Cheyenne and Sioux fled to nearby bluffs and counterattacked. The soldiers burned everything in camp, including robes and food they themselves could have used. However, when expected reinforcements did not arrive, the cavalry withdrew. Most families escaped, though hardly dressed for winter. The army rounded up six hundred ponies, but while the soldiers camped that night, the warriors stole them back. The attack accomplished little except to send the families north, where they joined the hostile Sioux.

Those fleeing families made their way on foot downstream to the location of Lakota Sioux leader Crazy Horse. The camp stood on the East Fork of the Little Powder River.[9] From there, the bands decided to combine and travel for common defense, hunting buffalo as they went. They made their way to Sitting Bull's village, sixty miles farther north on another branch of the Powder River. As they traveled northwest toward the Yellowstone River, those who had stayed at reservation agencies during the winter joined them for spring hunting. Smaller bands joined, too. There had been 360 lodges in

Sitting Bull's camp in mid-April. By early June there were 461.[10]

During April and May, while Terry and Custer prepared their arm of the campaign, Colonel Gibbon's troops camped on the north bank of the Yellowstone River. Gibbon's mission was to prevent hostiles from fleeing north. He then moved downstream and camped near the mouth of Rosebud Creek.

To the east, Terry and his Dakota Column, along with Custer and twelve companies of the Seventh Cavalry, searched for hostile camps. Sitting Bull's village had to move often. There was not enough grass in one location to feed the enormous herd of ponies, nor enough game for the families. Yet in spite of the village size, the tribes were hard to locate. The area was vast and the land swelled with benches and ravines. Finally army scouts reported spotting Sitting Bull's camp near the Little Missouri River. Terry sent Custer to verify the information.

Major Marcus Reno and six troops of Custer's regiment were also sent out to search for hostiles. They all met at the mouth of the Rosebud River.

Custer continued to the Powder River, leaving behind his marching band, some recruits, and the wagon train. Custer was getting down to business, leaving nonessentials behind. The troops then moved on up the Yellowstone to the mouth of the Tongue River, where Reno caught up with them. Reno reported finding signs of the enemy. Terry himself steamed up the Yellowstone River on the river steamer *Far West*.

The United States Army used the steamboat Far West *to transport troops and supplies.*

At different times during these movements, native scouts spotted soldiers north and south of them. It was then more than ever that the Native Americans believed that the government meant war. The army, simply, had come to kill them.

Sitting Bull grew convinced of this, too. With more Native Americans arriving in camp every day, Sitting Bull knew a general leadership was needed. Since he had been made head chief years earlier, he now took control.

The Sun Dance in Early June

The people looked to Sitting Bull for leadership. He was a holy man as well as a warrior. He, like other

Sioux, believed that the world was full of power. This energy might show itself in anything that was strange, wonderful, or strong, such as the sky, earth, animals, sun, and moon. The chief respected this power, which the Sioux called *Wakantanka*, the Great Mystery.[11] Sitting Bull asked for guidance from this power and promised, in prayer, a Sun Dance ceremony.

The Sun Dance was usually practiced every summer, in various ways by many Plains tribes. The bands would gather, give thanks to the Great Spirit, and ask for prosperity in the coming year.

The Sioux divided the ceremony into twelve days.[12] The first eight days were spent in festivities and preparation. Eventually those who would dance were separated from the others and given instructions from religious leaders. During that time, a special cottonwood tree was selected as the center pole for the ceremony.

The last four days were sacred. Women carried the sacred cottonwood tree to camp, where it was decorated and raised.

On the twelfth day, each warrior was painted according to the degree of pain he had agreed to suffer for the tribe. Each was also given an eagle-bone whistle, which he blew throughout the final dance.

Some warriors only fasted and danced. Others suffered having pieces of flesh cut from their bodies and thrown under the pole for sacrifice. Still others had wooden skewers or fasteners hooked under skin flaps, with heavy buffalo skulls attached. The ultimate torture was endured by those few who hung suspended from the sacred pole. They attached rawhide ropes to skewers that were hooked to skin flaps on their chests or backs.

All participants then danced while staring at the sun. The warriors had hope of receiving a vision from the Great Spirit while they endured their agony. The dance continued until each dancer's skin ripped free.

This year, Sitting Bull suffered fifty pieces of skin cut from each of his arms as his sacrifice.[13] It was during this Sun Dance that Sitting Bull received his vision about Bluecoats falling into camp. To the Sioux and their allies, this vision assured them of a great victory.

While Sitting Bull's village was growing, the soldiers were making their own plans to force the hostiles back to the reservations.

Battle at Rosebud Creek

In early summer, General Crook put the next phase of the campaign into operation. On his way north, he signed up a couple hundred Shoshone and Crow support warriors.[14] As Crook and his troops headed up the Rosebud Valley, enemy scouts secretly spotted them. On June 17, hundreds of Sioux and Cheyenne warriors, including Crazy Horse, rode out to meet them. Sitting Bull went with them; he did not fight, however, but called encouragement from the sidelines. His body was still sore from the Sun Dance ceremony the week before.[15]

As Crook's troops stopped for midmorning coffee

in a bowl-like area surrounded by bluffs, they heard shots from above. At the same time, their scouts rode into camp, shouting, "Sioux, Sioux!"[16]

Without waiting for orders, the soldiers fell in, and none too soon. Sioux ringed the bluffs above, shooting long-distance at the soldiers. Crook, who had 1,028 men at his command, kept seeing wave after wave of warriors charge at them. One observer said they looked like "swarms of blackbirds."[17]

For six hours the two sides fought. Combat was the type of guerrilla warfare the warriors fought so well.[18] Even though the Sioux were pushed back by the training and firepower of Crook's men, the Sioux fought with a fierceness the soldiers had not seen before.

Between the Sioux and Cheyenne, there were acts of shame and acts of bravery that day. The shame fell on Jack Red Cloud, Red Cloud's son. At one point in the battle, Jack's horse was shot from under him, and Jack fell off. Normally, to show scorn for the enemy, the warrior took time in the heat of combat to coolly retrieve the war bridle from his fallen horse. Jack did not do this, but panicked instead. His fellow warriors scorned him for that. Jack left the fighting and rode all the way back to his tribe's hunting area in northwestern Nebraska in shame.[19]

At another time during the battle, a Cheyenne chief, Comes in Sight, had his horse shot out from under him. He was surrounded by enemies and prepared to die. Just then another mounted Cheyenne swooped down, held out a hand, and the chief swung up behind the rider. They galloped to safety. The rider who saved the chief's life was his sister, Calf Trail Woman. In honor of this bravery, the Cheyenne always talked of the Rosebud encounter as the battle "Where the Girl Saved Her Brother."[20]

While the late afternoon approached on the Rosebud, fighting men and horses on both sides grew exhausted. Ammunition ran low. When Crook took a defensive position, the attackers withdrew and rode back to their camp.

Because the Sioux retreated, Crook declared a

Sioux Chief Spotted Eagle set up camp along the Tongue River, in 1879, in Montana Territory.

victory. It was not one, however. Crook's men were in bad shape; many wounded needed attention, and their supplies and ammunition were nearly gone. That meant probably six weeks before his troops could fight again. Crook needed reinforcements, and his men needed to recuperate before he could push on.

Instead of continuing to the Yellowstone, Crook had his wounded taken care of and considered his forces out of the battle. He was no longer part of the campaign, and the other army leaders did not know what had happened to him. How might this withdrawal affect the events to come?

The morning after the Rosebud battle, the Sioux and their allies moved camp, traveling down a fork of the Little Bighorn River and angling to the southwest. They made camp in the valley of the Greasy Grass, along the Little Bighorn River.

Sitting Bull knew the Rosebud battle was not the one to fulfill his vision. He watched during the following days and saw his camp grow still larger. In six days alone, the village had doubled: from three thousand to seven thousand people, from eight hundred to eighteen hundred fighting men.[21] Most of the camp included Sioux, Cheyenne, and a handful of Arapahos.[22] Some were survivors of Sand Creek. Some had taken flight from Minnesota after the massacre there. People had come together for the spring hunt, but their numbers, nevertheless, would be strong if they ran into trouble with the Bluecoats.

7

"A Good Day to Die"

On June 21, General Terry met with Colonel Gibbon and Custer on the Yellowstone River where the supply steamboat the *Far West* was moored. That afternoon, Terry, Gibbon, and Custer met in the cabin of the steamboat to plan their campaign.

The commanders only knew the approximate location of a large camp of hostiles. They assumed the tribes would scatter the moment they realized army troops were nearby. Therefore, the officers worried not about how to defeat the enemy, but how to trap them before they fled in every direction.[1]

Terry divided the forces. Custer and the Seventh Calvalry were to scout up the Rosebud. Terry and Gibbon would march up the Yellowstone to the mouth of the Bighorn, and then on to the Little Bighorn River. That way the Terry-Gibbon column would bar a northern and western escape, and Custer would bar an eastern escape. Crook, expected from Wyoming Territory, was to bar a southern escape.

It was during this meeting that Colonel Gibbon said he could not reach the mouth of the Little Bighorn River with his troops "before noon of the

26th."[2] No one was aware of Crook's defeat several days earlier. There had been no communication from his division.

The next day at noon, the Seventh Cavalry gathered before its officers near the banks of the Yellowstone River. Custer's band was not there, but brass trumpets rang out as the troops paraded before Commanding General Alfred Terry. Mounted by his side was Colonel John Gibbon and Lieutenant Colonel George Armstrong Custer.

Terry had offered Custer more men and two Gatling guns to take along in the search for the renegades. But Custer refused the extra help, knowing heavy artillery

Gatling guns were the first practical quick-firing machine guns used in the United States.

would slow his progress. Besides, he was sure his military command of about six hundred men could take on and win victory in any conflict with the hostile force.

Before leaving, Custer received general orders from Terry: to scout out various Cheyenne and Sioux bands south perhaps as far as the Tongue River, then turn west toward the Little Bighorn. Custer's troops would cut off the enemy from the east while Terry and Gibbon's troops blocked from the north. The fight that would soon engage Custer would be the single most important battle of these wars.[3]

The review finally over, Custer's Seventh moved out, heading south toward the headwaters of the Rosebud.

Custer's command counted 31 officers and 566 enlisted men. In addition, there were over thirty friendly Sioux, Arikara, and Crow scouts, packers, and guides and a few civilian employees. There was also a pack train with supplies and ammunition.

The Seventh Cavalry rode on for several days, searching for camps, often covering about thirty miles a day. At the same time, the troopers tried to keep their own whereabouts unknown. Finding anything on the grassy, rolling ridges of the Plains was difficult. Custer sent scouts ahead to look for signs, such as dust rising in the air caused by moving horses or smoke from tepee fires. They found the trail on June 23. The element of surprise could be a great advantage in a fight.

On the morning of June 24, army scouts located the site where the Sun Dance had been held earlier in the month. Several campsites were found. Grass nearby was cropped short from grazing village herds. Scouts knew these campsites were part of a huge camp that stretched for miles along the creek. From the signs, the scouts felt there would be more enemies in one band than had ever gathered before. And that meant more warriors, too. With the trail so fresh, Custer kept the troops moving under cover of night.

The dawn of Sunday, June 25, 1876, was clear and hot, and almost windless. Crow and Arikara scouts rode into Custer's camp bringing a message about a huge Sioux encampment ahead. They told of horses—twenty thousand or more—swarming over distant hills like a moving brown carpet.[4] Custer climbed to a high vantage point called the Crow's Nest, but he could not see the village.

Simultaneously, the scouts discovered Sioux braves watching from a distance. Once spotted, Custer had a decision to make: whether to attack or to wait for reinforcements.

The commander considered. His men were tired after the night march. He did not know the exact strength of the enemy or exactly where the camp was, and Terry had directed him to wait.

But if he waited, Custer reasoned, the long-sought enemies might break camp. They would flee in all directions. Then the regiment would never find them.

Custer decided to find the village and attack when possible.

By noon, the army troops were within striking distance at the head of a tributary later named Reno Creek. It was difficult to find out the exact enemy situation because a line of ridges rolled off to the distance, hiding valleys below.

Custer then divided his command. He sent Captain Frederick Benteen with his battalion (about one hundred twenty-five men) toward the south with orders to look for hostiles among the ridges. He was to continue west and north until he could see into the Little Bighorn Valley. His troops were then to rejoin the main column.

Custer assigned Companies A, G, and M (about 140 men) to Major Reno. To his own immediate command, Custer kept Companies E, F, C, I, and L (225 horsemen), then divided these into two battalions. Company B (129 strong) was to guard the pack train and bring up the rear.

After Benteen moved out, Custer's column proceeded down Reno Creek, with Reno's column on the left bank. The pack train, loaded with ammunition and supplies, soon fell behind.

By 2:15 P.M., after a march of ten miles, the columns figured they were within four miles of the village on the Little Bighorn River.

It was at that point the soldiers surprised a party of Sioux, who raced off toward the Little Bighorn. From the top of a knoll, Custer saw a column of dust

Marcus A. Reno, realizing that he did not have the support of Custer's men, ordered his troops to retreat to the edge of the Little Bighorn River.

to the north behind ridges. He was afraid the hostiles were breaking camp and getting away.

Immediately, Custer ordered Major Reno to take his column and charge forward, attacking the camp from the south. While Reno's troops caused that diversion, Custer and his remaining men (about 215) would swoop in and support Reno.[5] Reno's battalion rode off for the attack.

Reno's Column

Although alerted that enemy soldiers were scouting the area, Sitting Bull's village did not expect an attack right then. In the camps the women and children had been warned to be ready to move back away from the village. They were told that they would be guarded.

Crazy Horse prepared himself for battle. He painted a lightning streak across the side of his face and hail marks on his body. Suddenly, he heard the crack of gunfire far upstream. He sprang on his yellow pinto and chose a party of warriors to go with him.

But Crazy Horse did not enter the battle just then. Instead, he took his warriors and watched others fighting in the distance. He studied the numbers and watched the battle line. He sent and received messages from warriors in other parts of the battle.

At last Crazy Horse received a signal that another attacking force (Custer) was north, behind the ridges. Crazy Horse and Gall then turned down the valley. They rode through the village, gathering hundreds of warriors as they moved.

In another part of camp, Sitting Bull stepped from his tepee. He saw horses and Bluecoats through a tower of dust in the distance. Confusion reigned as women and children hurried away from camp and as warriors raced toward the fighting.

Reno, who had never fought Native Americans before, saw the rush of enemies pounding toward him in growing numbers. Alarmed, he looked back for the promised Custer support but saw none. He threw his hand up and ordered his troops to dismount and take a defensive position. Trooper William C. Slaper, a survivor of the battle and only twenty-one years old, later said:

> Rifle fire, and bullets began to whistle about us. . . . This was my first experience under fire. I know that for a time I was frightened, and far more so when I got my first glimpse of the Indians riding about in all directions, firing at us and yelling and whooping like incarnate fiends.[6]

Overwhelmed by warriors, Reno then retreated with the survivors along the bank of Little Bighorn River. Every fourth man grabbed the reins of his own horse and three others and led them to the rear. Into the timber they went, stretching a thin skirmish line partway across the valley. The warriors rode the length of the line and around the end, circling into the rear.

After fifteen minutes, Reno knew this position was not good. He ordered a retreat into the cottonwood groves. There the dense undergrowth and thick timber kept him from forming his men into any sensible defense. The Sioux worked through the brush, and Reno soon lost control of his companies.

In the confused next half hour, Reno ordered his men to mount the horses and dismount several times. Some soldiers heard, some did not. Noise, smoke, and fear washed through the grove.

Finally, at the edge of the woods, Reno managed to form a loose column, and he led it in fast retreat up the valley. The hostiles galloped among the panicking men, picking off troopers at will. When the troopers reached the river, warriors gathered at the bank and fired at the soldiers who struggled to cross the water.

Cheyenne war chief Two Moon later remembered the moment: "Indians covered the flat. They began to drive the soldiers all mixed up—Sioux, then soldiers, then more Sioux, and all shooting. The air was full of smoke and dust. I saw the soldiers fall back and drop into the river-bed like buffalo fleeing."[7]

The soldiers made their way through the ravines up to the bluffs. Only 100 of the 140 men remained, exhausted and beaten.[8] Some were wounded. No sooner had this remnant reached the heights of the bluffs than the enemy pulled back. This was lucky for Reno, but, as it turned out, unlucky for Custer.

Custer's Last Stand

While Reno's fight was going on, Crazy Horse had waited and prepared himself for battle. The warriors were surprised there were so few Bluecoats attacking such a large camp. Perhaps, they thought, these battles were only diversions, and other soldiers were on their way.

What happened to Custer and his column on that fateful afternoon cannot be known. From various pieces of evidence, however, historians have sketched the story.

To that point, it is believed, Custer had still not seen the huge village. Custer's Arikara and Crow scouts knew what was coming.[9] They had read the signs, seen the trail, seen the huge pony herd, and seen the smoke from maybe thousands of lodges far in

George Armstrong Custer with three scouts and one guide

the distance. A Crow army scout, Half Yellow Face, had earlier turned to Custer and said, "You and I are both going home today by a road we do not know."[10] Custer learned that the warriors were not fleeing, but were coming out to meet the soldiers. If Custer had planned to follow Reno's column into battle, he now changed his mind. As yet, Custer was not sure what was happening with his other battalions.

When Custer finally reached a northern bluff overlooking the Sioux camp after 3:00 P.M., the full situation revealed itself.[11] Below in the distance, for three miles, tepees were scattered along the tree-lined Little Bighorn River. Reports later estimated fifteen hundred to two thousand Plains warriors encamped in the village. That was three or more times the total strength of the Seventh Cavalry, and at least twice the number expected by the army.

One of Custer's Crow scouts recalled seeing camps and camps and camps below. Another scout remembered, "We could see Reno fighting. He had crossed the creek. Everything was a scramble with lots of Sioux."[12]

Custer continued the march on the north side, below the crest of the bluffs, and then down through a narrow ravine. He knew then he needed help. He wanted Benteen's support, and he was worried about ammunition. Custer sent for the pack train.

One message was sent to Benteen for aid, and then another. Benteen was south, perhaps five miles away. Custer swung around to his trumpeter, Giovanni

Captain Frederick Benteen led his troops to the south to prevent the Native Americans from escaping.

Martini, and said, "Orderly, I want you to take a message to Colonel Benteen. Ride as fast as you can and tell him to hurry."[13] Officer William Cooke scrawled the orders down in a note: "Benteen. Come on. Big Village. Be Quick. Bring packs. W. W. Cooke. P. bring packs."[14]

Below, Crazy Horse rode through camp, collecting warriors as he went. They raised their rifles high in the air and shouted the traditional battle cry: "Hoka hey, Lakotas! It's a good day to die!"[15] Crazy Horse, joined by Gall, headed toward Custer's battalion.

At the same time, Custer and his men were moving up a bank opposite the village. Before they made it across the river to attack the village, waves of warriors beat against them. The warriors were soon reinforced by warriors from Reno's battle. The

THE BATTLE OF THE LITTLE BIGHORN—June 25, 1876

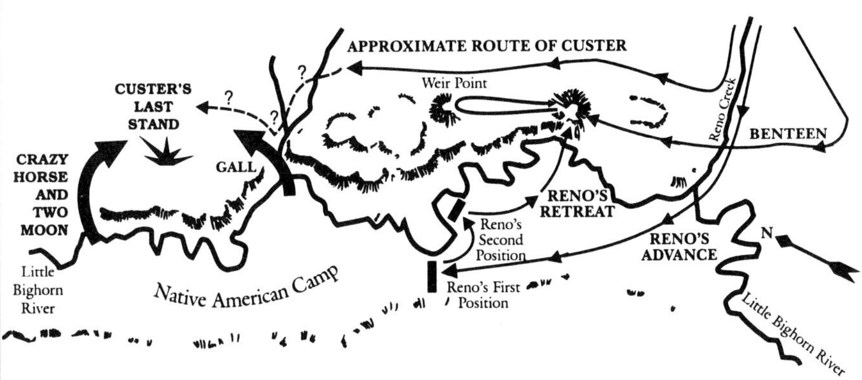

This map illustrates the various routes the soldiers used to reach the Little Bighorn River.

SOURCE DOCUMENT

This pictographic account of the Battle of Little Bighorn by the Sioux Red Horse is titled, "Custer's column fighting."

soldiers were pushed back and strung out in the open, being cut down by warriors led by Crazy Horse and Gall. Most of the troopers' horses had been driven off.

Chief Two Moon, the Cheyenne leader, described the conflict:

> The whole valley was filled with smoke, and the bullets flew all around us, making a noise like bees . . . When the guns were firing, the Sioux and Cheyennes and soldiers, one falling one way and one falling another, together with the noise of the guns.[16]

Eventually, all five of Custer's companies were forced back, fighting in groups from Calhoun Hill and Medicine Tail Ford, each company making its own "last stand." Chief Gall pressed from the front,

Crazy Horse from the rear. Troopers laid down a heavy fire, keeping the warriors at bay. After about forty-five minutes, the soldiers withdrew.

Chief Gall kept after the enemy. Captain Myles Keogh dismounted, struggling with his men up Battle Ridge above the far side of the village.

Now the warriors fired at the soldiers handling the horses. Enough horse handlers died and enough horses stampeded that Keogh's men ended largely on foot. Carbine ammunition packs went with the horses, and the soldiers threw the carbines away and grabbed their pistols. They struggled to the southern end of Battle Ridge, where they joined Captain George Yates and his men.

While Keogh's men were fighting Gall, Custer and Yates kept up fire with Crazy Horse from the north. Crazy Horse swept down Little Bighorn Valley, forded the river, and climbed Battle Ridge. "There were so many of us," said Lakota Black Elk, "that I think we did not need guns. Just the hoofs would have been enough."[17] An Oglala woman viewing the battle scene recalled, "The Indians acted just like they were driving buffalo to a good place where they could be easily slaughtered."[18]

Survivors of these companies—about forty men—gathered around the banner of Custer's headquarters at the northern end of Battle Ridge. The soldiers fought among the smoke, grime, dust, and noise of battle. The harassed men shot their horses and used them as protective barriers. They fought until they were all killed. This stand at Little Bighorn was over in about two hours. Every soldier in Custer's immediate battalion was gone, dead on the grass above the Little Bighorn River.

When was Custer killed? Most accounts place him along the battle ridge on Last Stand Hill. However, one account by army Crow scout Goes-ahead said it was near the beginning of the last stand battle:

> He [Custer] went "*ahead,*" rode "*into the water of the Little Bighorn,*" with Two-bodies [probably Custer's guide, Mitch Boyer] on one side of him, and his flag on the other—and he "*died*" there, "*died in the water of the Little Bighorn,*" with Two-bodies, and the blue soldier carrying his flag.[19]

Some people believe Custer's body was then carried to the hill, where it was later found.

The victorious warriors galloped around the

SOURCE DOCUMENT

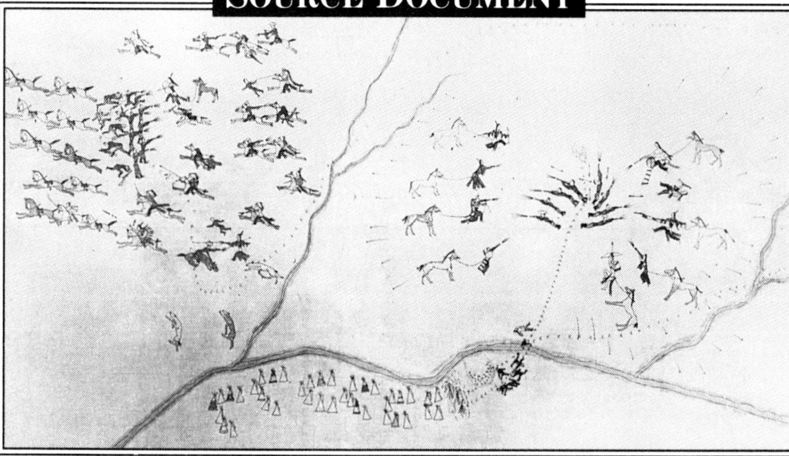

A Cheyenne's interpretation of the Battle of Little Bighorn. Drawing by White Bird.

battlefield, killing wounded men, raising great clouds of dust. The women and children made their way up from the village to rob and mutilate the bodies.[20]

Continued Attacks on Reno

Meanwhile, four miles up the river, Reno's men dug in, still struggling to survive. Nearly half of his command was either missing, dead, or wounded.[21] Benteen's battalion, some dozen miles back on the trail, received the first urgent message for support from Custer. Soon after, Martini rode up, his horse bleeding from a gunshot in the hip, with the second order for help. When Benteen received the note from Custer, he ordered a steady run to help.

Benteen reached the Little Bighorn just in time to see the last of Reno's men struggling from the valley. A Crow scout appeared and pointed to the high bluffs where Reno's survivors gathered. After a short gallop, Benteen found Reno and reinforced his troops. Reno said to his fellow officer, "For God's sake, Benteen, halt your command and help me. I've lost half my men."[22]

No one knew where Custer was or what was happening. Noise of firing guns drifted down from the north, but neither commander left to investigate. Either they had too many wounded or they could not decide what to do.

Finally done with Custer and his battalion, the triumphant warriors turned toward Reno's surviving forces and Benteen's troops. The enemy pushed the soldiers up toward the north slopes. The companies had dug in around the hill, now called Weir Point, but soon fell back. Lieutenant Edward Godfrey knew the danger of panic retreat, and he with Company K held the enemy back while the rest of the command secured the bluff top. Surviving horses and pack mules were herded into a depression in the ground, and they offered some protection to the soldiers and the wounded.

There, under constant attack, the Reno-Benteen forces held out for three hours. When it was dark, the fighting stopped. The cavalry men dug in during the night, Major Reno on guard at the north end and Benteen at the south.

There was no victory dance in the village that night. The tribes had lost warriors, too. Instead, there was mourning for the dead. The many wounded needed care.

In Stanley Vestal's book *Sitting Bull*, Sitting Bull is reported to have said, "My heart is full of sorrow that so many were killed on each side, but when they compel us to fight, we must fight."[23]

At dawn on June 26, fighting resumed with no letup. From all sides, arrows and bullets rained into the army defenses on the bluff top. A couple of times the soldiers under Benteen and Reno made short charges to drive back the pressing enemy.

The besieged soldiers were tormented by thirst. At one point, sharpshooters provided cover so a few soldiers could sneak down to the river and fill canteens. They obtained little water, but it was enough.

Sitting Bull remained in the village until noon, and then he returned to the heights to observe the fighting on the bluff, where the army held out.

Finally Sitting Bull told his warriors, "Let them go now so some can go home and spread the news. I just saw some more soldiers coming."[24] Native American scouts indeed had come back to the village with news that more soldiers were on the way. By early afternoon, their gunfire slackened.

In the valley, the warriors set fire to the dry prairie grass and a wall of thick smoke hid the camps. By 7:00 P.M., a procession of tribes, with their goods, wound from the valley toward the Big Horn Mountains. Except for scattered debris, the valley was soon deserted.

Would Rescue Come?

Up on Reno Hill, the surviving soldiers gazed down into the deserted valley. No one knew what had happened. Where was Custer? Would the enemy return? The soldiers held their position.

The next morning—June 27—the soldiers saw a blue column coming from the distance up the valley. Was it Custer? Could it be Terry, or even Crook? Two officers rode out and found Terry had arrived from the north. Gibbon was in the area, too. Still no one had news of Custer.

Four miles downstream, Colonel Gibbon's chief of

scouts had already found the dead on Battle Ridge. Gibbon brought news of the Custer deaths. No one believed it could happen. Custer, with all his luck, was dead. Lieutenant Charles Varnum said, "The idea of Custer's command having been all killed never entered my mind."[25]

Lieutenant Godfrey, who survived with the Reno troops, remembered climbing to the highest point with a few men, where the whole field came into view. It was the first sight they had had of the battlefield. "What are those?" asked several soldiers as they pointed at what looked like white boulders in the distance. Peering through field glasses, Godfrey replied, "The Dead!" A mounted colonel nearby said, "Oh, how white they look! How white!"[26]

Many dead troopers had been mutilated. The soldiers found Custer's body among his dead comrades. The general had two bullet holes in him, but he was not mutilated.[27]

However, Kate Bighead, a Cheyenne who had been at Washita as a young girl, gave another account after the battle. She said two Cheyenne women came to Long Hair's body on the battlefield and punctured his eardrums with a pointed sewing tool. Custer had been told years earlier in Oklahoma if he ever made war on the Cheyenne again, he would be killed. He did not listen. With punctured eardrums, he would hear better in the afterlife.[28]

Soldiers found the only army survivor of Custer's immediate command—Captain Keogh's horse,

Comanche—not far from the broken bodies. (There may have been a regimental dog that lived, and perhaps several other wounded horses, too.[29]) The survivor was a fourteen-year-old bay and in bad shape. The men managed to get him to the stables at Fort Abraham Lincoln, where they supported the horse in a sling while he healed. In April 1878, Comanche was made "second commanding officer" of the Seventh Cavalry. Whenever he walked in parades later, Comanche was draped in black mourning net. As was the custom for a military horse whose owner died in battle, a pair of cavalry boots was slung across the saddle with the toes pointing backward.[30]

Captain Myles Keogh's horse, Comanche. Gustave Korn took care of Comanche after Captain Keogh was killed.

The dead soldiers of the Little Bighorn battle were buried where they fell. The wounded were transported down the Yellowstone and the Missouri rivers to the town of Bismarck aboard the steamboat *Far West*. Then they were helped to Fort Abraham Lincoln.[31]

As for the Sioux, Sitting Bull's vision had been fulfilled. Enemy bluecoats had "fallen into camp."

Four nights later, farther down the valley, the various tribes gathered to observe their victory. "They celebrated the greatest triumph the Sioux and Cheyennes had ever known . . . over any enemy white or Indian."[32]

The Sioux and Cheyenne had won the battle not because of leadership. Native Americans fought in an individual, guerrilla-like fashion with little formal leadership. A fighting man followed a chief into combat because he wanted to, not because he was directed to.

The warriors won because they outnumbered the soldiers three to one; because their families were in immediate danger; and because they were united, sure of themselves, and angry.[33]

But the great triumph of this battle was, at the same time, the end of Sioux and Cheyenne power as truly free people. When the news spread to white communities, a flood of hatred washed over the West. And with it, a renewed determination that the "savages" be tamed.

8

Public Fury After the Battle

The headline in the July 6, 1876, issue of the *Bismarck Tribune Extra* read, "MASSACRED GEN. CUSTER AND 261 MEN THE VICTIMS."[1] If George Custer wanted fame and popularity, he had them now. The white defeat and Custer's death, rang in the United States' centennial year with national mourning.

That sensational article, the first to come from the actual area, was reprinted all over the East. The newspaper told of the battle, focusing on the mutilations, the overpowering force of the enemy, and the calm bravery of the soldiers. What information the editors did not have, they made up. Use of words like "slaughter" and "red devil" shocked and inflamed millions of readers. The public reacted with grief at first, and then outrage. Not since Abraham Lincoln's assassination, some said, had the country grieved so.[2]

After that, white people cried for revenge. All over the country, volunteers wanted the honor of trailing the "savages" and bringing them to justice. Volunteer groups sprang up in cities from east to west. Even in Custer's hometown of New Rumley, Ohio, the

SOURCE DOCUMENT

FIRST ACCOUNT OF THE CUSTER MASSACR

TRIBUNE EXTRA.

Price 25 Cents. BISMARCK, D. T., JULY 6, 1876.

MASSACRED

GEN. CUSTER AND 261 MEN THE VICTIMS.

NO OFFICER OR MAN OF 5 COMPANIES LEFT TO TELL THE TALE.

3 Days Desperate Fighting by Maj. Reno and the Remainder of the Seventh.

Full Details of the Battle.

LIST OF KILLED AND WOUNDED.

THE BISMARCK TRIBUNE'S SPECIAL CORRESPONDENT SLAIN.

Squaws Mutilate and Rob the Dead

Victims Captured Alive Tortured in a Most Fiendish Manner.

What Will Congress Do About It?

Shall This Be the Beginning of the End?

It will be remembered the the Bismarck Tribune sent a special correspondent with Gen. Terry, who was the only professional correspondent with the expedition. Kellogg's last words to the writer were: "We leave the Rosebud tomorrow and by the time this reaches you we will have

MET AND FOUGHT.

the red devils, with what result remains to be seen. I go with Custer and will be at the death." How true! On the morning of the 22d Gen. Custer took up the line of march for the trail of the Indians, reported by Reno on the Rosebud. Gen. Terry, apprehending danger, urged Custer to take additional men, but Custer having full confidence in his men and in their ability to cope with the Indians in whatever force he might meet them, declined the proffered assistance and marched with his regiment alone. He was instructed to strike the trail of the Indians, to follow it until he discovered their position, and report by courier to Gen. Terry whowould reach the mouth of Little Horn by the evening of the 26th, when he would act in concert with Custer in the final wiping out. At four o'clock, the afternoon of the 24th, Custer scouts reported the location of a village recently deserted, whereupon Custer went intocamp, marching again at 11 p. m., continuing the march until daylight, when he again went into camp for coffee. Custer was then fifteen miles from the village located on the Little Horn, one of the branches of the Big Horn, twenty miles above its mouth, which could be seen from the top of [illegible] divide, and after lunch General Custer pushed on. The Indians by this time had discovered his approach and soon were seen mounting in great haste, riding here and there, it was presumed in full retreat. This idea was strengthened by finding a freshly abandoned Indian camp with a deserted tepee, in which one of their dead had been left, about six miles from where the battle took place. Custer with his usual vigor pushed on making seventy-eight miles without sleep, and attacked the village near its foot with companies C, E, F, I, and L, of the seventh cavalry, Reno having in the mean time attacked it at its head with three companies of cavalry which, being surrounded, after a desperate hand to hand conflict, in which many were killed and wounded, cut their way to a bluff about three hundred feet high, where they were reinforced by four companies of cavalry under Col. Benteen. In gaining this position Col. Reno had to recross the Little Horn, and at the ford the hottest fight occurred. It was here where Lieutenants McIntosh, Hodgson [illegible] Sioux, emptying several chambers of his revolver, each time bringing a red-skin before he was brought down—shot through the heart. It was here Bloody Knife surrendered his spirit to the one who gave it, fighting the natural and hereditary foes of his tribe, as well as the foes of the whites.

The Sioux dashed up beside the soldiers in some instances knocking them from their horses and killing them at their pleasure. This was the case with Lt. McIntosh, who was unarmed except with a saber. He was pulled from his horse, tortured and finally murdered at the pleasure of the red devils. It was here that Prof. Girard was separated from the command and lay all night with the screeching fiends dealing death and destruction to his comrades within a few feet of him, and, but time will not permit us to relate the story, through some means succeeded in saving his fine black stallion in which he took so much pride. The ford was crossed and the summit of the bluffs, having, Col. Smith says, the steepest sides that he ever saw ascended by a horse or mule, reached, though the ascent was made under a galling fire.

The companies engaged in this affair were those of Captain Boylan, French and McIntosh. Col. Reno had gone ahead with these companies in obedience to the order of Gen. Custer, fighting most gallantly, driving back repeatedly the Indians who charged in their front, but the fire from the bluff being so galling, forced the movement heretofore alluded to. Signals were given and soon Benteen with the four companies in reserve came up in time to save Reno from the fate with which Custer about this time met. The Indians charged the hill time and again but were each time repulsed with heavy slaughter by its gallant defenders. Soon, however, they reached bluffs higher than those occupied by Reno, and opened a destructive fire from points beyond the reach of cavalry carbines. Nothing being heard from Custer, Col. Weir was ordered to push his command along the bank of the river in the direction he was supposed to be, but he was soon driven back, retiring with difficulty. About this time the Indians received strong reinforcements, and litterally swarmed the hill sides and on the plains, coming so near at times that stones were thrown into the ranks of Col. Reno's command by those unarmed or out of ammunition. Charge after charge in quick succession, the fight being sometimes almost hand to hand. But they drew off finally, taking to the hills and ravines. Col. Benteen charged a large party in a ravine, driving them from it in confusion. They evidently trusted in their numbers and did not look for so bold a movement. They were within range of the corral and wounded several packers, J. C. Wagoner, among the number, in the head, while many horses and mules were killed. Near 10 o'clock the fight closed, and the men worked all night strengthening their breastworks, using knives, tin cups and plates, in place of spades and picks, taking up the fight again in the morning. In the afternoon of the second day the desire for water became almost intolerable. The wounded were begging piteously for it; the tongues of the men were swollen and their lips parched, and from lack of rest they were almost exhausted. So a bold attempt was made for water. Men volunteered to go with canteens and camp kettles, though to go was almost certain death. The attempt succeeded though in making it one man was killed and several wounded. The men were relieved, and that night the animals were watered. The fight closed at dark, opening again next morning, and continuing until the afternoon of the 27th. Meantime the men become more and more exhausted and all wondered what had become of Custer. A panic all at once was created among the Indians and they stampeded, from the hills and from the valleys, and the village was soon deserted except for the dead. Reno and his brave band felt that succor was nigh. Gen. Terry came in sight, and strong men wept upon each others necks but [illegible] word was had from Custer. Hand skaking and congratulations were scarcely over when Lt. Bradley reported that he had found Custer dead, with one hundred and ninty cavalry men. Imagine the effect. Words cannot picture the feeling of these, his comrades and soldiers. Gen. Terry sought the spot and found it to be too true. Of those brave men who followed Custer, all perished; no one lives to tell the story of the battle. Those deployed as skirmishers, lay as they fell, shot down from every side, having been entirely surrounded in an open plain. The men in the companies fell in platoons, and like those on the skirmish line, lay as they fell, with their officers behind them in there proper positions. General Custer, who was shot through the head and body, seemed to have been among the last to fall, and around and near him lay the bodies of Col. Tom and Boston, his brothers, Col. Calhoun, his brother-in-law, and his nephew, young Reed, who insisted on accompaning the expedition for pleasure. Col. Cook and [illegible] ies terribly mutilated. The squaws seem to have passed over the field and crushed the skulls of the wounded and dying with stones and clubs. The heads of some were severed from the body, the privates of some were cut off, while others bore traces of torture, arrows having been shot into their private parts while yet living, or other means of torture adopted. The officers who fell were as follows: Gen. G. A. Custer, Cols. Geo. Yates, Miles Keogh, James Calhoun, W. W. Cook, Capts. McIntosh, A. E. Smith, Lieutenants Riley, Critenden, Sturgis, Harrington, [illegible] and Porter, Asst. Surgeon DeWolf. The only citizens killed were [illegible] Custer, Mr Reed, Charles Reynolds, Isiah, the interperter from Ft. Rice and Mark Kellogg, the latter the Tribune correspondent. The body of Kellogg alone remained unstriped of its clothing, and was not mutilated. Perhaps as they had learned to respect the Great Chief, Custer, and for that reason did not mutilate his remains they had in like manner learned to respect this humble shover of the lead pencil and to that fact may be attributed this result. The wounded were sent to the rear some fourteen miles on horse litters striking the Far West sixty odd miles up the Big Horn which point they left on Monday at noon reaching Bismark nine hundred miles distant at 10 p. m.

The burial of the dead was sad work but they were all decently interred. Many could not be recognized; among the latter class were some of the officers. This work being done the [illegible] way back to the base where Gen. Terry, awaits supplies and approval of his plans for the future campaign.

The men are worn out with marching and fighting, and are almost wholly destitute of clothing.

The Indians numbered at least eighteen hundred lodges in their permanent camp, while those who fought Crook seems to have joined them, making their effective fighting force nearly four thousand. These were led by chiefs carrying flags of various colors, nine of whom were found in a burial tent on the field of battle. Many other dead were found on the field, and near it ten squaws at one point in the ravine—evidently the work of Ree or Crow scouts.

The Indian dead were great in number, as they were constantly assaulting an inferior force. The camp had the appearance of being abandoned in haste. The most georgeous ornaments were found on the bodies of the dead chiefs, and hundreds of finely dressed and painted robes and skins were thrown about the camp. The Indians were certainly severely punished.

We said of those who went into battle with Custer none are living—one Crow scout hid himself in the field, and witnessed and survived the battle. His story is plausable, and is accepted, but we have not room for it now. The names of the wounded are as follows:

LIST OF WOUNDED.

Private Davis Corey, Co. I, 7th Cav, right hip; Patrick McDonnall, D, left leg; Sergt. John Paul, H, back; Priv. Michael C. Madden, K, right leg; Wm. George, H, left side, died July 3d, at 4 a. m.; 1st Sergt. Wm. Heyn, A, left knee; Pvt. John McVay, C, hips; Patrick Corcoran, K, right shoulder; Max Wilke, K, left foot; Alfred Whitaker, C, right elbow; Peter Thompson, C, right hand; Jacob Deal, A, face; J. H. Meyer, M, back; Roman Rutler, M, right shoulder; Daniel Newell, M, left thigh; Jas. Muller, H, right thigh; Elijah T. Stroude, A, right leg; Sergt. Patrick Carey, M, right hip; Privt. James E. Benett, C, body, died July 5th, at 3 o'clock; Francis Reeves, A, left side and body; James Wilbur, M, left leg; Jasper Marshall, L, left foot; Sergt. James T. Riley, E, back and left leg; Privt. John J. Phillips, H, face and both hands; Samuel Severn, H, both thighs; Frank Brunn, M, face and left thigh; Corpl. Alex B. Bishop, H, right arm; Privt James Foster, A, right arm; W. E. Harris, M, left breast; Chas. H. Bishop, H, right arm; Fred Homsted, A, left wrist; Sergt Chas. White, M, right arm; Privt [illegible] M, right [illegible]; Chas. Campbell, [illegible] right shoulder; John Cooper, H, right elbow; John McGuire, C, right arm; Henry Black, H, right hand; Daniel McWilliams, H, right leg.

An Indian scout, name unknown, left off at Birthold; Sergt M. Riley, Co. I, 7th Infantry, left off at Buford, Consumption; Privt David Ackison, Co. E, 7th cav., left off, July 4th, at Buford, Constipation.

The total number of killed was two hundred and sixty one; wounded 52. Thirty-eight of the wounded were brought down on the Far West; three of them died en route. The remainder are cared for at the field hospital.

De Rudio had a narrow escape and his escape is attributed to the noise of beavers, jumpng into the river during the engagement. De Rudio followed them, got out of sight, and after hiding for twelve hours or more finally reached the command in safety.

The body of Lt Hodgson did not fall into the hands of the Indians; that of Lt McIntosh did [illegible] was badly mutilated. McIntosh, though a half-breed, [illegible] Gen. Custer, Cols. Calhoun, Yates, Capt. Smith, and Lt. Porter. The unhappy Mrs. Calhoun, loses a husband three brothers and a nephew. Lt. Harrington also had a family, but no trace of his remains was found. We are indebted to Col. Smith for the following full list of the dead; to Dr. Porter for the list of wounded, which is also full.

KILLED.

Field and staff, George A. Custer, Brevt. Major General.

W. W. Cook, Brevt. Lt-Colonel.

Lord, Asst. Surgeon, J. M. DeWolf, Acting Asst. Surgeon.

N. C. Staff, [illegible] Sharrow, Serg Major.

Henry Voss, Chief Insptr.

A Henry Dallans .... Corp.
" G. K. King .... "
" J. E. Armstrong .... Privt
" James Drinaw .... "
" Wm. Moody .... "
" R. Rowlins .... "
" James McDonald .... "
" John Sullivan .... "
" Thos. P. Switzer .... "
B Benj. Hodgson .... 2d Lieut
" Richard Doran .... Privt
" George Mask .... "
C T. W. Custer .... Brevt Lt-Col
" H. M. Harrington .... 2d Lt

The body of Lt. Harrington was not found, but it is reasonably certain that he was killed.

" Edwin Baba .... 1st Sergt
" Finley .... Sergt
" Finkle .... "
" French .... Corpl
" Foley .... "
" Ryan .... "
" Allen .... Privt
" Criddle .... "
" King .... "
" Bucknell .... "
" Eisman .... "
" Engle .... "
" Brightfield .... "
" Fanand .... "
" Griffin .... "
" Hamel .... "
" Hattisoll .... "
" Kingsoutz .... "
" Lewis .... "
" Mayer .... "
" Mayer .... "
" Phillips .... "
" Russell .... "
" Rix .... "
" Ranter .... "
" Short .... "
" Shea .... "
" Shade .... "
" Stuart .... "
" St. John .... "
" Thadius .... "
" Van Allen .... "
" Warren .... "
" Windham .... "
" Wright .... "
D Vincent Charley Farrier
" Patrick Golden .... Privt
" Edward Hansen .... "
E A. E. Smith .... Brevt Capt
" E. Sturgis .... 2d Lt

The body of Lt. Sturgis was not found, but it is reasonably certain he was killed.

" F. Hohmeyer .... 1st Sergt
" Egnen .... Sergt
" James .... "
" Hagan .... Corp
L James Calhoun .... 1st Lt
" Miller .... Privt
" Tweed .... "
" Veller .... "
" Cashan .... "
" Kiefer .... "
" Andrews .... "
" Crisfield .... "
" Harnington .... "
" Haugge .... "
" Kavaugh .... "
" Lobering .... "
" Mahoney .... "
" Schmidt .... "
" Lunon .... "
" Semenson .... "
" Riebold .... "
" O'Connell .... "
" J. J. Crittenden .... 20th Inf
" Butler .... 1st Sergt
" Warren .... "
" Harrison .... Corpl
" Gilbert .... "
" Seiller .... "
" Walsh .... Teptr
" Adams .... Privt
" Assdely .... "
" Burke .... "
" Cheever .... "
" McGue .... "
" McCartiy .... "
" Dugan .... "
" Maxwell .... "
" Scott .... "
" Babcock .... "
" Perkins .... "
" Tarbox .... "
" Dye .... "
" Tessler .... "
" Galvin .... "
" Graham .... "
" Hamilton .... "
" Rodgers .... "
" Snow .... "
" Hughes .... "
K D. Whitney .... 1st Sergt
" Hughes .... Sergt
" J. J. Callahan .... Corpl
" Julius Helmer .... Trptr
" Eli U. T. Clair .... Privt
I M. W. Keogh .... Col
" J. E. Porter—the body of Lt. Porter was not found, but it is reasonably certain he was killed.
" F. E. Varden .... 1st Sergt
" J. Burtard .... "
" Jonn Wild .... Corpl
" G. C. Morris .... "
" H. A. Bailey .... Blacksmith
" J. E. Broadhurst .... Privt
" J. Barry .... "
" J. Conners .... "
" T. P. Downing .... "
" Mason .... "
" Blorm .... "
" Meyer .... "
" McElroy .... Trptr
" Mooney .... "
" Baker .... Privt
" Boyle .... "
" Barth .... "
" Conner .... "
" Daring .... "
" Davis .... "
" [illegible] .... "
" Hiley .... "
" Huber .... "
" Hince .... "
" Henderson .... "
" Henderson .... "
" Leddisson .... "
" O'Conner .... "
" Rood .... "
" Reese .... "
" Smith 1st .... "
" Smith 2nd .... "
" Smith 3rd .... "
" Stella .... "
" Stafford .... "
" Schoole .... "
" Smallwood .... "
" Tarr .... "
" Vaugant .... "
" Walker .... "
" Bragew .... "
" Knight .... "
F G. W. Yates .... Capt
" W. Van Rieley .... 2d Lt
" Kenney .... 1st Sergt
" Nursey .... Sergt
" Vickey .... "
" Wilkinson .... "
" Coleman .... Capt
" Feeman .... "
" Briody .... "
" Brandon .... Farrier
" Manning .... Blacksmith
" Atchison .... Privt
" Brown 1st .... "
" Brown 2nd .... "
" Bruce .... "
" Brady .... "
" Burnham .... "
" Cather .... "
" Carney .... "
" Dohman .... "
" Donnelly .... "
" Gardiner .... "
" Hammon .... "
" Kline .... "
" Krianth .... "
" Luman .... "
" Losse .... "
" Milton Jas .... "
" Madson .... "
" Monroe .... "
" Ruddew .... "
" Omeling .... "
" Sicfous .... "
" Sanders .... "
" Wanew .... "
" Way .... "
" Lerock .... "
" Kidey .... "
" E. C. Driscoll .... "
" D. C. Gillette .... "
" C. H. Gross .... "
" F. P. Holcomb .... "
" M. E. Horn .... "
" Adam Hitiamer .... "
" P. Killey .... "
" Fred Lehman .... "
" Henry Lehman .... "
" E. P. Lloyd .... "
" A. Mclchargey .... "
" J. Mitchell .... "
" [illegible] .... "
" J. O'Bryan .... "
" J. Parker .... "
" F. J. Pitter .... "
" Geo. Post .... "
" Jas. Quinn .... "
" Wm. Reed .... "
" J. W. Rossberg .... "
" D. L. Lymons .... "
" J. E. Troy .... "
" Chas. Van Bramer .... "
" W. B. Whaley .... "
G Daniel McIntosh .... 1st Lt
" Edward Botzer .... Sergt
" M. Considine .... "
" Jas Martin .... Capt
" Otto Hageman .... "
" Benj. Wells .... Farrier
" Henry Dose .... Trptr
" Crawford Selby .... Saddler
" Benj. F. Rodgers .... Privt
" Andrew J. Moore .... "
" Jno. J. McGinniss .... "
" Edward Stanley .... "
" Henry Seafferman .... "
" John Papp .... "
H Geo. Lee .... Corpl
" Julian D. Jones .... Privt
" Thos. E. Meador .... "
M Miles F. O'Hara .... Sergt
" Henry M. Scollier .... Corpl
" Fred Stringer .... "
" Henry Gordon .... Privt
" H. Klotzbursher .... "
" G. Lawrence .... "
" W. D. Meyer .... "
" G. E. Smith .... "
" D. Somers .... "
" J. Tanner .... "
" H. Tenley .... "
" H. C. Voyt .... "
Boston Custer .... Civilian
Arthur Reed .... "
Mark Kellogg .... "
Chas. Reynolds .... "
Frank C. Mann .... "

INDIAN SCOUTS.

Bloody Knife
Bobtailed Bull.
Stab.

Total number of Commissioned officers killed 14
Actg asst Surg 1

The first newspaper account of the Little Bighorn Battle was in the Bismarck Tribune Extra, *July 6, 1876.*

first-grade students swore oaths to kill Sitting Bull on sight.[3]

Placing the Blame

Throughout history, people have debated about why the army lost the battle. A national hero had died, and people felt responsibility had to be placed somewhere.

All the major army officers of the campaign came under blame at one time or another: Terry for not gathering enough information before the fight; Gibbon for not keeping Terry informed; Crook for withdrawing his troops before the campaign; Benteen for not coming to Custer's aid fast enough during the battle. Custer himself received much of the blame for not following Terry's intentions, for attacking with exhausted men, and for not seeing the enemy he was facing beforehand. He was also blamed for dividing his forces.[4]

Marcus Reno, however, became the live scapegoat. Many labeled him a coward for not pushing the attack on the village. Others said that once his forces were defending their position on the bluff, he should have rallied to Custer's defense whatever possible disaster. Reno's critics said he failed to be an effective commander.

Reno called for an army court of inquiry, which began January 13, 1879. He was eventually cleared, but the tarnish stayed with him until his death.

One strong Custer defender proved to be Libbie Custer. Any criticism against her husband or his tactics was quickly countered. She spent the rest of her life writing about her Autie and defending him. She died in New York City on April 6, 1933, two days shy of her ninety-first birthday.[5]

Historian Robert Utley gave his own view of the outcome of the battle and the various leaders who were blamed. "It is easy to do injustice to the responsible commanders. One cannot know fully all the . . . factors . . . that . . . shaped the final outcome."[6] In any case, the Native Americans were many that day, and they fought well: In simple terms, the army lost because the Sioux and Cheyenne won.

With the defeat at Little Bighorn in 1876, the government and army forces pressed to clear up the Native American problem. Officials expanded military troops out West. General Crook marched with purpose and drove his men. Columns of soldiers rallied and bent to the task, burning tribal villages, killing warriors, and destroying food supplies until an uneasy truce prevailed.

General George Crook later became head of the Division of the Missouri, with headquarters in Chicago. Although he spent most of his life fighting Native Americans, he spent his last years fighting for their rights. He died on March 21, 1890, in Chicago.

After the Sioux victory at Little Bighorn in 1876, Sitting Bull and his followers fled to Canada, where they lived peacefully for four years. However, because of dwindling food sources there, Sitting Bull brought his people back to the United States. With the buffalo nearly gone and his people starving, Sitting Bull surrendered at Fort Buford, North Dakota, in the summer of 1881.

Several years later, entertainer Buffalo Bill Cody persuaded the now famous Sitting Bull to tour the United States and Canada with the Wild West Show. The chief told a reporter that he enjoyed show business, but he missed the fresh air of the prairie.[7]

Crazy Horse also lived a free life after the Little Bighorn Battle, but only for a year. In the face of growing white numbers and power, Crazy Horse finally surrendered at Camp Robinson, Nebraska, and to reservation life in 1877. Later that year, officials heard rumors that Crazy Horse planned to stir up trouble. They ordered him locked up in the guardhouse at Camp Robinson. While resisting entering a jail cell there, a soldier bayoneted Crazy Horse, and he later died. He was only thirty-five years old.

For fifteen years after Little Bighorn, the Sioux lived quietly. One treaty violation by the government led to another until Congress forced the Native Americans to sell land sought by white settlers. Of the nearly four hundred treaties drawn up from 1776 to 1871, more than half concerned Native American lands—most of them reducing the amount of land a tribe possessed.[8] The Sioux were confined to the Great Sioux Reservation, South Dakota. Reservation life, along with white attempts to "civilize" the Sioux, left them bitter and hopeless.

From the Pine Ridge Agency, South Dakota, Red Cloud proved invaluable to his people during those

Sitting Bull toured the United States and Canada with Buffalo Bill Cody, in his Wild West Show. This photo of the two was taken in 1885.

trying times after the Little Bighorn battle. He was a chief who knew the reality of government power. Because of this, he became a diplomatic intermediary, extracting favorable compromises for his people from the government and giving as little away as possible.[9]

By the mid-1880s, there were 187 reservations in the United States. These were home to 243,000 Native Americans.[10] And five years later, in February 1890, the Sioux accepted a land agreement. An additional 9 million acres of land were opened to white settlement.[11]

To many Sioux, this was the blackest moment in their history. They were starving and their people were dying of epidemics of measles, flu, and whooping cough.

The Ghost Dance and Wounded Knee

Beginning in 1889, Native Americans in the west heard of a religious ceremony called the Ghost Dance. It began as a vision from Wovoka, a Paiute born in 1856, who became a medicine man in Nevada. Wovoka had a vision in 1889 that a messiah would come to save them. That by dancing and preparing the mind, "one day soon the earth would tremble and the whites would be washed away. The dead Indians would return, and with them the buffalo herds."[12]

For those who loved the old way of life, the Ghost Dance was a miracle. Until then, "There was no hope on earth," Red Cloud said, "and God seemed to have forgotten us."[13]

Dakota dancing the Ghost Dance, before the Battle at Wounded Knee.

Soon the Ghost Dance religion spread from Native American agency to agency. The followers wore special Ghost Dance shirts, which they believed could not be penetrated by bullets.

The United States government grew alarmed at the tribal response to the Ghost Dance. Finally white leaders banned dancing. Fearing such activity would cause riot or revolt, officials arrested several leaders. It was during such an arrest that Sioux policemen murdered Sitting Bull at his camp at Grand River, South Dakota.

The Seventh Cavalry (some were the same soldiers

from Reno's and Benteen's commands who had survived the Battle of the Little Bighorn[14]) headed by Colonel James W. Forsyth was sent to pursue Sioux leader Big Foot and his Ghost Dance followers. The military brought along four cannon to strengthen their force.

Soldiers caught up with the fleeing Ghost Dance band while they camped at Wounded Knee Creek in South Dakota. On December 29, 1890, the soldiers were posted around the camp. Forsyth ordered the Sioux to turn over their weapons. Both sides were edgy. When one warrior shot a soldier, the Seventh opened fire.

There was brutal hand-to-hand fighting on each side. When the cannon fired from a nearby hill, the killing took everyone in its path. More than one hundred fifty men, women, and children fell that day—a true massacre, as most were unarmed.[15] The magical power of the Ghost Dance shirts had not protected their believers.

"And so it was all over," Lakota Black Elk said. "And I can see that something else died there in the bloody mud, and was buried in the blizzard. A person's dream died there. . . . There is no center any longer, and the sacred tree is dead."[16]

Except for a few skirmishes after Wounded Knee, the wars of the West were over.

The Native American frontier might have been lost, in the symbolic sense, before this last battle. For on December 17, 1890, two weeks before Wounded

Sitting Bull and his family at Fort Randall, Dakota Territory. From left to right: Her Holy Door (mother), Good Feather (sister), Sitting Bull, Walks Looking (daughter), Has Many Horses (daughter), and Tom Fly (grandson).

Knee, a Sioux was buried in a rough wooden box at Fort Yates, North Dakota, near the Standing Rock Agency. Wrapped in canvas in the coffin were the remains of the one man who might well have represented unyielding Native American independence.

It was Sitting Bull.

★ Timeline ★

1842—First wagons cross Sioux country on the Oregon Trail.

1848—*January 24*: Gold is discovered in Sutter's Creek, California.

1851—*September 23*: Treaty of 1851 at Fort Laramie, Wyoming, is signed by the United States and the Plains tribes.

1854—*August 19*: John Grattan's command at Fort Laramie, Wyoming, is destroyed by warriors when Grattan opens fire on a Sioux village.

1857—*Summer*: Lakota Sioux hold their first grand council. The Sioux pledge to keep white people from their land.

1857—*August 28*: Fort Abercrombie is established in North Dakota to protect settlers in the Red River Valley from Sioux attacks.

1860—*April*: The first riders of the Pony Express carry mail from Missouri to California in ten days.

1861—The United States Civil War begins.

1862—John Bozeman establishes a trail through the northern Plains to the gold diggings in Montana.

1862—*May 20*: The Homestead Act is signed by President Abraham Lincoln. This act makes public land available for citizens and their families.

1862—*July 1*: The Pacific Railway Act is signed by Congress, allowing the construction of a transcontinental railroad.

1862—*August*: The Santee rebel and massacre over four hundred white settlers. Some Santee are punished by the United States government and some flee west to Sitting Bull's camp.

1864—*September 28*: Peaceful Cheyenne and Arapaho tribes meet with Colorado governor John Evans and Colonel John Chivington, and say they will keep peace and move near forts.

1864—*November 29*: Colonel John Chivington and his volunteer army massacre peaceful Cheyenne and Arapaho at Sand Creek, Colorado.

1865—*April 9*: The Civil War officially ends.

1866—*Summer*: Three forts are built along the Bozeman Trail to protect white travelers.

1866—*December 21*: Fetterman Fight between soldiers and Lakota warriors takes place outside Fort Phil Kearny, Wyoming.

1867—*August 2*: Wagon Box Fight erupts outside Fort Phil Kearny between soldiers and Lakota.

1867—*September*: A government peace commission meets with nine bands of Sioux at North Platte, Nebraska.

1868—*April*: Treaty of 1868 is negotiated at Fort Laramie between the Sioux/Cheyenne and the United States government.

1868—*Summer*: The Bozeman forts are abandoned.

1868—*Fall*: General Philip Sheridan begins a winter campaign against Cheyenne and Sioux warriors in Colorado and Indian Territory.

1868—*November 27*: Washita massacre takes place in Indian Territory [Oklahoma].

1873—Richest gold and silver strike in history of mining is discovered near Virginia City, Nevada.

1874—*July*: Custer and the Seventh Calvary make an expedition into the Black Hills, South Dakota, where they discover gold.

1875—Government officials try to buy or lease the Black Hills, but the Sioux refuse.

1876—Federal officials insist that all Sioux report to reservations by January 31 or face military action.

1876—*March 17*: General George Crook's forces attack a Cheyenne village. Most Cheyenne flee north to the camp of Crazy Horse.

1876—*May 17*: General Alfred Terry and Lieutenant Colonel George Custer leave Fort Abraham Lincoln to begin a plan to crush the Sioux and Cheyenne.

1876—*Early June*: Sioux perform the Sun Dance.

1876—*June 17*: Sioux and Cheyenne attack General Crook's troops at Rosebud Creek.

1876—*June 25*: The Battle of the Little Bighorn takes place.

1877—*February 28*: A Congressional Act takes the Black Hills and ends all Sioux rights outside the Great Sioux Reservation.

1881—*July 19*: Sitting Bull and his followers return to the United States from Canada and surrender at Fort Buford, Dakota Territory.

1889—The Ghost Dance religion gains Native American support.

1890—*December 15*: Sitting Bull is killed by Native American police at his cabin on the border between North and South Dakota.

1890—*December 29*: Army troops massacre over three hundred Sioux at Wounded Knee, South Dakota.

1891—*January 15*: The Sioux formally surrender at White Clay Creek, Nebraska.

1909—*December 10*: Red Cloud dies at the age of eighty-seven on the Pine Ridge Agency, South Dakota.

★ Chapter Notes ★

Chapter 1

1. Stanley Vestal, *Sitting Bull: Champion of the Sioux* (Norman, Okla.: University of Oklahoma Press, 1957), pp. 148–151.

2. Leslie Tillett, ed., *Wind on the Buffalo Grass* (New York: Thomas Y. Crowell Company, 1976), p. xiv.

3. Russell Thornton, *American Indian Holocaust and Survival: A Population History Since 1492* (Norman, Okla.: University of Oklahoma Press, 1987), p. 43.

Chapter 2

1. Benjamin Capps, *The Indians* (Alexandria, Va.: Time-Life Books, 1973), p. 45.

2. James A. Maxwell, ed., *America's Fascinating Indian Heritage* (Pleasantville, N.Y.: Reader's Digest Association, Inc., 1978), p. 157.

3. Russell Freedman, *Buffalo Hunt* (New York: Holiday House, 1988), p. 38.

4. Stanley Vestal, *Sitting Bull: Champion of the Sioux* (Norman, Okla.: University of Oklahoma Press, 1957), p. 14.

5. Capps, p. 69.

6. Carl Waldman, *Encyclopedia of Native American Tribes* (New York: Facts on File, 1988), pp. 222–223.

7. Thomas B. Marquis, *Keep the Last Bullet for Yourself* (New York: Reference Publications, Inc., 1976), p. 59.

8. Robert M. Utley, *Custer Battlefield* (Washington, D.C.: U.S. Government Printing Office, 1987), p. 40.

9. Robert M. Utley and Wilcomb E. Washburn, *Indian Wars* (Boston: Houghton Mifflin Company, 1977), p. 172.

10. Capps, pp. 153–154.

11. Ibid.

12. John R. Howard, *Awakening Minorities* (New Brunswick, N.J.: Transaction Books, 1970), p. 15.

Chapter 3

1. Benjamin Capps, *The Indians* (Alexandria, Va.: Time-Life Books, 1973), p. 163.

2. Robert M. Utley and Wilcomb E. Washburn, *Indian Wars* (Boston: Houghton Mifflin Company, 1977), p. 167.

3. James A. Maxwell, ed., *America's Fascinating Indian Heritage* (Pleasantville, N.Y.: Reader's Digest Association, Inc., 1978), p. 192.

4. Edward Lazarus, *Black Hills White Justice* (New York: HarperCollins Publishers, 1991), p. 16.

5. Utley and Washburn, *Indian Wars*, p. 169.

6. Charles J. Kappler, ed., *Indian Treaties 1778–1883* (New York: Interland Publishing, Inc., 1972), p. 595.

7. Lazarus, p. 17.

8. Donald E. Worcester, *Forked Tongues and Broken Treaties* (Caldwell, Idaho: Caxton Printers, Ltd., 1975), p. xx.

9. Utley and Washburn, *Indian Wars*, p. 168.

10. Capps, p. 169.

11. Worcester, p. 126.

12. Maxwell, p. 193.

13. Evan S. Connell, *Son of the Morning Star* (San Francisco: North Point Press, 1984), p. 65.

14. Lazarus, p. 22.

15. Ibid., p. 24.

16. *New Encyclopedia Britannica* (Chicago: University of Chicago Press, 1993), p. 731.

17. John R. Milton, *Crazy Horse* (Minneapolis: Dillon Press, Inc., 1974), Introduction.

18. Utley and Washburn, *Indian Wars*, p. 211.

19. Lazarus, p. 25.

20. Keith Wheeler, *The Railroaders* (New York: Time-Life Books, 1973), p. 21.

Chapter 4

1. Edward Lazarus, *Black Hills White Justice* (New York: HarperCollins Publishers, 1991), p. 27.

2. Benjamin Capps, *The Indians* (Alexandria, Va.: Time-Life Books, 1973), p. 175.

3. Ibid., p. 170.

4. Robert M. Utley, *The Lance and the Shield* (New York: Henry Holt and Company, 1993), p. 115.

5. Lazarus, p. 35.

6. Capps, p. 184.

7. Robert M. Utley and Wilcomb E. Washburn, *Indian Wars* (Boston: Houghton Mifflin Company, 1977), p. 206.

8. Ibid.

9. David Nevin, *The Soldiers* (Alexandria, Va.: Time-Life Books, 1974), p. 147.

10. James A. Maxwell, ed., *America's Fascinating Indian Heritage* (Pleasantville, N.Y.: Reader's Digest Association, Inc., 1978), p. 195.

11. Capps, p. 187.

12. Utley and Washburn, *Indian Wars*, p. 207.

13. Maxwell, p. 196.

14. Utley and Washburn, *Indian Wars*, p. 207.

15. Capps, p. 186.

16. Donald E. Worcester, *Forked Tongues and Broken Treaties* (Caldwell, Idaho: Caxton Printers, Ltd., 1975), p. 136.

17. Lazarus, p. 36.

18. Worcester, p. 242.

19. Nevin, p. 136.

20. Ibid., p. 137.

21. Evan S. Connell, *Son of the Morning Star* (San Francisco: North Point Press, 1984), p. 131.

22. Nevin, p. 140.

23. Lazarus, p. 39.

24. Ibid.

25. Utley, *The Lance and the Shield*, p. 71.

26. Cyrus Townsend Brady, *Indian Fights and Fighters* (Lincoln, Nebr.: University of Nebraska Press, 1971), p. 68.

27. Thomas B. Marquis, *Keep the Last Bullet for Yourself* (New York: Reference Publications, Inc., 1976), p. 148.

28. Brady, pp. 68–69.

29. Lazarus, p. 46.

30. Ibid.

31. Nevin, p. 143.

32. Russell Freedman, *Indian Chiefs* (New York: Holiday House, 1987), p. 23.

Chapter 5

1. James A. Maxwell, ed., *America's Fascinating Indian Heritage* (Pleasantville, N.Y.: Reader's Digest Association, Inc., 1978), p. 199.

2. Ibid., p. 201.

3. Robert M. Utley and Wilcomb E. Washburn, *Indian Wars* (Boston: Houghton Mifflin Company, 1977), p. 215.

4. Edward Lazarus, *Black Hills White Justice* (New York: HarperCollins Publishers, 1991), p. 48.

5. Robert M. Utley, *The Lance and the Shield* (New York: Henry Holt and Company, 1993), p. 82.

6. Utley and Washburn, *Indian Wars*, p. 217.

7. Stanley Vestal, *Sitting Bull: Champion of the Sioux* (Norman, Okla.: University of Oklahoma Press, 1932), pp. 108–109.

8. Lazarus, p. 52.

9. Benjamin Capps, *The Indians* (Alexandria, Va.: Time-Life Books, 1973), p. 190.

10. Evan S. Connell, *Son of the Morning Star* (San Francisco: North Point Press, 1984), p. 183.

11. Robert M. Utley, *Cavalier in Buckskin: George Armstrong Custer and the Western Military Frontier* (Norman, Okla.: University of Oklahoma Press, 1988), p. 67.

12. Cyrus Townsend Brady, *Indian Fights and Fighters* (Lincoln, Nebr.: University of Nebraska Press, 1971), p. 164.

13. Utley and Washburn, *Indian Wars*, p. 223.

14. Lazarus, p. 59.

15. Ibid.

16. Capps, p. 200.

17. Lazarus, p. 61.

18. Ibid., p. 64.

19. John F. Finerty, *War-path and Bivouac: The Big Horn and Yellowstone Expedition* (Lincoln, Nebr.: University of Nebraska Press, 1966), p. xxvi.

20. "Cavalry Program," pamphlet from Little Bighorn Battlefield National Monument, Montana.

21. Thomas B. Marquis, *Keep the Last Bullet for Yourself* (New York: Reference Publications, Inc., 1976), p. 51.

22. Lazarus, p. 74.

23. Connell, p. 18.

24. Ibid., p. 247.

25. Frederick E. Hosen, *Rifle, Blanket and Kettle* (Jefferson, N.C.: McFarland, 1985), pp. 129–130.

26. Kenneth Hammer, ed., *Custer in '76: Walter Camp's Notes on the Custer Fight* (Provo, Utah: Brigham Young University Press, 1976), p. 20.

Chapter 6

1. Geoffrey Barraclous, ed., *The Times Atlas of World History* (Maplewood, N.J.: Hammond, Inc., 1978), p. 220.

2. *World Almanac 1995* (Mahwah, N.J.: World Almanac, 1994), p. 376.

3. Russell Thornton, *American Indian Holocaust and Survival: A Population History Since 1492* (Norman, Okla.: University of Oklahoma Press, 1987), p. xvii.

4. Robert M. Utley, *The Lance and the Shield* (New York: Henry Holt and Company, 1993), p. 128.

5. Robert M. Utley, *Custer Battlefield* (Washington, D.C.: Government Printing Office, 1988), p. 26.

6. David Nevin, *The Soldiers* (Alexandria, Va.: Time-Life Books, 1974), p. 173.

7. Utley, *The Lance and the Shield*, p. 139.

8. Edward Lazarus, *Black Hills White Justice* (New York: HarperCollins Publishers, 1991), p. 86.

9. Utley, *Custer Battlefield,* pp. 32 33.

10. Utley, *The Lance and the Shield*, p. 134.

11. Ibid., p. 2.

12. James A. Maxwell, ed., *America's Fascinating Indian Heritage* (Pleasantville, N.Y.: Reader's Digest Association, Inc., 1978), pp. 189–191.

13. Stanley Vestal, *Sitting Bull: Champion of the Sioux* (Norman, Okla.: University of Oklahoma Press, 1932), pp. 149–150.

14. Robert M. Utley and Wilcomb E. Washburn, *Indian Wars* (Boston: Houghton Mifflin Company, 1977), p. 237.

15. Utley, *The Lance and the Shield*, p. 141.

16. Cyrus Townsend Brady, *Indian Fights and Fighters* (Lincoln, Nebr.: University of Nebraska Press, 1971), p. 194.

17. Ibid.

18. "The Way West," part 4, *American Experience* video.

19. James Welch and Paul Stekler, *Killing Custer* (New York: W.W. Norton & Company, 1994), p. 121.

20. Ibid.

21. Utley, *The Lance and the Shield*, p. 142.

22. Utley, *Custer Battlefield,* p. 44.

Chapter 7

1. Robert M. Utley, *Custer Battlefield* (Washington, D.C.: Government Printing Office, 1988), p. 37.

2. Cyrus Townsend Brady, *Indian Fights and Fighters* (Lincoln, Nebr.: University of Nebraska Press, 1971), p. 266.

3. David Nevin, *The Soldiers* (Alexandria, Va.: Time-Life Books, 1974), p. 199.

4. Ibid., p. 211.

5. James A. Maxwell, ed., *America's Fascinating Indian Heritage* (Pleasantville, N.Y.: Reader's Digest Association, Inc., 1978), p. 200.

6. E.A. Brininstool, *Troopers with Custer: Historic Incidents of the Battle of the Little Bighorn* (Lincoln, Nebr.: University of Nebraska Press, 1952), p. 48.

7. Robert M. Utley, *The Lance and the Shield* (New York: Henry Holt and Company, 1993), p. 152.

8. Brininstool, pp. 55–57.

9. Nevin, p. 209.

10. Evan S. Connell, *Sun of the Morning Star* (San Francisco: North Point Press, 1984), p. 274.

11. Douglas McChristian, Chief Historian, Little Bighorn Battlefield National Monument, April, 1995.

12. Utley, *Custer Battlefield,* p. 58.

13. Brininstool, p. 189.

14. Utley, *Custer Battlefield,* p. 61.

15. Benjamin Capps, *The Indians* (Alexandria, Va.: Time-life Books, 1973), p. 217.

16. Leslie Tillett, ed., *Wind on the Buffalo Grass* (New York: Thomas Y. Crowell Company, 1976), p. 95.

17. John G. Neihardt, *Black Elk Speaks* (Lincoln, Nebr.: University of Nebraska Press, 1961), p. 116.

18. Utley, *The Lance and the Shield*, p. 156.

19. Frank B. Linderman, *Pretty-Shield* (Lincoln, Nebr.: University of Nebraska Press, 1932), p. 236.

20. Robert M. Utley, *Cavalier in Buckskin: George Armstrong Custer and the Western Military Frontier* (Norman, Okla.: University of Oklahoma Press, 1988), p. 191.

21. Robert M. Utley and Wilcomb E. Washburn, *Indian Wars* (Boston: Houghton Mifflin Company, 1977), p. 244.

22. Utley, *Custer Battlefield,* p. 69.

23. Stanley Vestal, *Sitting Bull: Champion of the Sioux* (Norman, Okla.: University of Oklahoma Press, 1932), p. 174.

24. Utley, *The Lance and the Shield*, p. 160.

25. Thomas B. Marquis, *Keep the Last Bullet for Yourself* (New York: Reference Publications, Inc., 1976), p. 180.

26. John E. Parsons and John S. du Mont, *Firearms in the Custer Battle* (Harrisburg, Pa.: The Stackpole Company, 1953), p. 52.

27. Utley and Washburn, *Indian Wars*, p. 247.

28. Evan S. Connell, *Son of the Morning Star* (San Francisco: North Point Press, 1984), p. 422.

29. Ibid., p. 295.

30. Ibid., p. 297.

31. Utley, *Custer Battlefield,* pp. 73–74.

32. Utley, *The Lance and the Shield*, p. 160.

33. Ibid., pp.161–162.

Chapter 8

1. D.T. Bismarck, "Tribune Extra" in James Welch and Paul Stekler, *Killing Custer* (New York: W.W. Norton and Company, 1994), p. 191.

2. Edward Lazarus, *Black Hills White Justice* (New York: HarperCollins, 1991), p. 89.

3. Ibid.

4. Robert M. Utley, *Custer Battlefield* (Washington, D.C.: Government Printing Office, 1988), pp. 83–89.

5. "Mrs. Custer Dead In Her 91st Year," *The New York Times,* April 5, 1933, p. 19.

6. Utley, *Custer Battlefield,* p. 89.

7. Robert M. Utley, *The Lance and the Shield* (New York: Henry Holt and Company, 1993), p. 265.

8. Donald E. Worcester, *Forked Tongues and Broken Treaties* (Caldwell, Idaho: Caxton Printers, Ltd., 1975), p. xix.

9. Utley, *The Lance and the Shield*, p. 249.

10. Robert M. Utley and Wilcomb E. Washburn, *Indian Wars* (Boston: Houghton Mifflin Company, 1977), p. 290.

11. Worcester, p. 316.

12. Ibid., p. 317.

13. Lazarus, p. 113.

14. Benjamin Capps, *The Great Chiefs* (Alexandria, Va.: Time-Life Books, 1975), p. 115.

15. Utley and Washburn, *Indian Wars*, pp. 299–300.

16. John G. Neihardt, *Black Elk Speaks* (Lincoln, Nebr.: University of Nebraska Press, 1979), p. 270.

★ Further Reading ★

Blumberg, Rhoda. *The Great American Gold Rush*. New York: Bradbury Press, 1989.

Brill, Marlene Targ. *The Trail of Tears: The Cherokee Journey from Home*. Brookfield, Conn.: Millbrook Press, Inc., 1995.

Fisher, Leonard Everett. *The Oregon Trail*. New York: Holiday House, 1990.

Freedman, Russell. *Buffalo Hunt*. New York: Holiday House, 1988.

———. *The Life and Death of Crazy Horse*. New York: Holiday House, 1996.

Hoig, Stan. *The Cheyenne*. New York: Chelsea House, 1989.

Lasky, Kathryn. *The Bone Wars*. New York: Morrow Junior Books, 1988.

Lawlor, Laurie. *Shadow Catcher*. New York: Walker and Company, 1994.

Levinson, Nancy Smiler. *Turn of the Century*. New York: Lodestar/Dutton/Penguin, 1994.

Miller, Brandon Marie. *Buffalo Gals*. Minneapolis: Lerner, 1995.

Reef, Catherine. *Buffalo Soldiers*. New York: Twenty-First Century Books, 1993.

Sandoz, Mari. *The Horsecatcher*. Lincoln. Nebr.: University of Nebraska Press, 1957.

Urwin, Gregory J.W. *The United States Cavalry*. Dorset, England: Blandford Books, 1983.

Wangerin, Walter, Jr. *The Crying for a Vision*. New York: Simon & Schuster, 1994.

★ INDEX ★